75 YEARS
OF BALLS

IMPERIAL POONA YACHT CLUB

By the same author:

A Hundred Years of Sailing at Oxford University (1984)
25 More Years of Sailing at Oxford University (2009)
75 Years of Port & Balls (2009)
Captivated by Sailing (2012) – editor
Golden Lily (2016) – editor
Introduction to Racing Companion (2019)

75 YEARS OF BALLS

THE HISTORY OF THE

IMPERIAL POONA YACHT CLUB

By The Gully Gully Man

(A.K.A. Jeremy Atkins)

SELF
PUBLISHING
HOUSE

Copyright © 2020 Jeremy Atkins

The right of Jeremy Atkins to be identified as the author of this work has been asserted by him in accordance with the Copyright, Designs and Patents Act 1988.

First published as part of 75 Years of Port & Balls, February 2009.
This edition published in 2020.
By Jeremy Atkins, The Windmill, Mill Lane, Harbury, Leamington Spa, Warwickshire, CV33 9HP, United Kingdom.
Created using services provided by Self Publishing House.

All rights reserved. No part of this publication may be reproduced, stored in a retrieval system or transmitted, in any form or by any means, electronic, mechanical, photocopying, recording, scanning or otherwise, except under the terms of the Copyright, Designs and Patents Act 1988 or under the terms of a licence issued by The Copyright Licensing Agency Ltd, Saffron House, 6-10 Kirby Street, London EC1N 8TS, UK, without the permission in writing of the Publisher.

ISBN: 9780950917955 (paperback); 9780950917948 (eBook)

CONTENTS

	Page
Forward (rather than Backward)	1
Sir Reginald Bennett, V.R.D. (1911 – 2000)	3
The Context	7
The First Incarnation	8
The Second Incarnation	18
Overseas Expansion	25
Developments at Home	31
Prince Philip & His Pot	42
Raids on Deauville	53
Back In Blighty	60
The New Millennium	70
Flag Officers	74

ACKNOWLEDGEMENTS

The task of writing the bizarre history of the Imperial Poona Yacht Club when I had only been a member of the club for less than half its 75 years was a challenge. But Reggie Bennett kept impressive records, including a Minute Book till the early 1950s, and a stack of photographs which have allowed many pictures in the Poona history. Unfortunately printing in black and white does not do justice to the bright colours (yellow and red) seen at any Poona event!

I am very grateful to many individuals who have helped in the production of the history, including:

Harry Anderson	Belinda Hadden	Jyotsna Shahane
Brian Appleton	Peter Hunter	Ed Smith
Lady Henrietta Bennett	Anthony Lunch	
Prof Sir Malcolm Green	Prince Philip	

I would also like to record my grateful thanks to a number of publications and publishers for the material that I have reproduced:

American Sailor Magazine	Tatler Magazine
Daily Mail Newspaper	Three Chousing Reers! (Reggie Bennett's memoir)
Field Magazine	
Guardian Newspaper	Times Newspaper
Independent Newspaper	Yachts & Yachting Magazine

Considerable effort has been made to trace copyright holders but if any has been inadvertently overlooked the author will be pleased to make the necessary arrangements at the first opportunity.

FORWARD

(RATHER THAN BACKWARD)

BUCKINGHAM PALACE.

It is undoubtedly true that life is a serious business, but that does not mean that it has to be taken seriously all the time. The Imperial Poona (Pune – in newspeak) Yacht Club is, in many senses of the word, a standard yacht club, but it is also, what might be termed, an anti-yacht club, founded by the arch anti-serious hero, Reginald Bennett.

I am delighted that the Gully Gully Man has undertaken to compose an account of the club's first 75 years. I believe that he has successfully met the challenge to combine historical accuracy while contending with the outrageous and the absurd. It is true that all the members are serious yachtsmen, in the sense that they are all rather good at it, but, what is equally important is that they all share a keen appreciation of the value of anti-seriousness. If you can bring yourself to read this book from cover to cover, you will be in a position to judge for yourself whether, or not, life can be significantly improved by not taking it too seriously all the time.

The Maharajah of Cooch Parwani

SIR REGINALD BENNETT, V.R.D.
(1911 – 2000)

It is only appropriate to start with the Club's leading light. The following obituary, written by John Barnes, appeared in The Independent on 28th December 2000 and is reprinted by kind permission of The Independent, Obituaries.

Reginald Bennett was a psychiatrist by profession, a yachtsman who represented Britain in international races against America and was unlucky never to take part in the Olympics, a long-serving Conservative MP and a thoroughly nice man.

His penetrating intellect and popularity in the House should have secured him a ministerial post but, at a time when MPs were expected to take life and themselves seriously, his inability to conform denied him the chance that he richly deserved. Had Iain Macleod lived, it is more than possible that Bennett, whom he understood well, might have found a place in the Government's ranks. But in reality it was too late. It was said that his prowess as a helmsman did him no favours with Heath, but his whole style was out of keeping with that of his leader and, just as he backed Macleod, until the latter dropped out of the leadership race, he would have felt far more at home in a party led by Reggie Maudling.

As one of his opponents, Tam Dalyell, observes, "There is an awful temptation for people to become caricatures of themselves in the House of Commons and he rather played at being the bon viveur to the extent that it damaged his chances of being taken seriously." Later entries in Dod's Parliamentary Companion solemnly record him as Chevalier du Tastevin 1971, de St Etienne (Alsace) 1972, de Bretvin (Muscadet) 1973, Commander de Bontemps-Medoc 1959. That tells its own tale. But in addition to chairing the Catering sub-committee of the House of Commons Services Committee from 1970 to 1974, he had chaired the Parliamentary Scientific Committee from 1958 to 1962, and that too should be remarked.

Born in Sheffield in 1911, the son of a civil servant, Reggie Bennett won scholarships to both Winchester and New College, Oxford, where he read Physiology, before completing his medical training in London at St George's Hospital and the Maudsley. It was his proud boast that he had qualified as a pilot in the University Air Squadron before he learnt to drive a car and he subsequently joined the London Division of the Royal Naval Volunteer Reserve. As a Surgeon Lieutenant-Commander he served first in Western Approaches and then with the Northern Patrol. He twice survived being torpedoed. He gained his wings with the Fleet Air Arm in 1941 and served first in Tanganyika and then in Ceylon. He was awarded the Volunteer Reserve Decoration in 1944.

At Oxford he had been awarded his Blue for sailing for each year from 1931 until 1934, the year in which he sailed for Britain against Germany at the Kiel Regatta and won the City of Hamburg Cup. In 1934 and 1935 he took the helm of Sir Richard Fairey's J-Class yacht Shamrock V in the races against the United States, but was reserve for the 1936 Olympics. Had the Second World War not intervened it is likely that he would have taken part in the 1940 Olympics. From 1936 until 1938 he raced the 12-metre Evaine and, after the War, represented Britain in the

British-American Cup races in 1949 and 1953. By then he was a Conservative MP and helped found the House of Commons Yacht Club, eventually serving as its Commodore.

He had been adopted for Woolwich East in 1937 and had contested it unsuccessfully in 1945. He was elected for Gosport and Fareham in 1950 and continued to represent the seat until it was divided. From February 1974 until he retired from the Commons in 1979 he represented Fareham. He served as Parliamentary Private Secretary to the Home Secretary from 1951 until 1954 and to the Minister of Fuel and Power, 1954-55, before being invited by Iain Macleod to become his PPS in 1955. "As someone who's had two ministers shot from under you," Macleod scribbled, "I wonder if you would consider coming and looking after me."

The two had met in the late 1940s when Macleod was at the Conservative Research Department and Bennett had offered to brief the party on health. Fond, some would say excessively so, of the camaraderie and gossip of the smoking room, he proved to be an ideal pair of ears and eyes for his minister, not least when Macleod was in deep trouble with the right of his party as Colonial Secretary from 1959 to 1961.

A shrewd judge of fellow Members, he warned Macleod during the leadership contest in 1963 that the choice would fall on the Foreign Secretary, Lord Home. According to Bennett, this news was greeted with total disbelief, but nevertheless in the early hours of 12 October, with Bennett serving "long thin scotches", Macleod briefed two of the leading political correspondents that Home was in the running. Bennett would never say, and may not have known, whether this was part of a bid to stall the leading candidates in mid-fight, so enabling a younger candidate to come through.

In the end, "quixotically" in Bennett's opinion, Macleod told Home to his face why he should not be Prime Minister and, unable to serve, retired to the back benches. Had he run in 1965, Bennett would have been among those organising his candidature, but his public denunciation of the "magic circle" that had picked Home had denied him any chance of victory.

It was at Bennett's invitation that Macleod joined the Thursday Club, which met over lunch at Wheeler's Restaurant in Soho to drink Chablis and establish the proposition that the weekend was about to begin. Later this involved the so-called Wessex Hunting Club, an occasion for foolery and hard drinking. Prince Philip was a member of the Thursday Club and was later invited to join the Imperial Poona Yacht Club, founded by Bennett when at Oxford for the purpose of challenging current undergraduates to take part in a backwards sailing race down the Thames.

There was a more serious side to him. As a young MP he became *a member of the Inner Temple and took a great interest in the affairs of the Medico-Legal Society. He spoke several languages including Arabic, Swahili and Italian, and chaired the Anglo-Italian Parliamentary Group for nine years. He wrote "Why Executives Die Young" in 1953 and "Psychological Disturbances of Young Married Life" in 1954 as well as medical pamphlets. He took an interest in polio research and the effect of polluted seawater, making the memorable comment that swimming in the Solent was "not so much swimming as going through the motions".*

Three years ago he published a memoir, "Three Chousing Reers".

THE CONTEXT

The earnest endeavour of the founders of the Oxford & Cambridge Sailing Society, recounted in the other part of this volume shows an enthusiastic, but perhaps somewhat arrogant attitude (inviting themselves to sail other people's boats) which was present at Oxbridge in the 1930s.

These were the early years of Brideshead Revisited – the time when Charles Ryder first met Sebastian Flyte at Oxford – the First World War a fading memory and no thought of another European conflict. Britain ruled the waves and the sun never set on the Empire.

A posting in India was common for many a profession, whether it be soldier, policeman, civil servant or whatever. In India, the British lived a privileged existence, and some found it hard to return to Blighty and settle back into a less exotic life. And, perhaps after too much time in the sun, they just wished to tell everyone they met about life in India.

Sir Reginald Bennett paints the picture in his memoir 'Three Chousing Reers':

In those days England was full of retired bigwigs from the Indian Army, the Civil Service and so forth who all reminisced at length. A chap called Sir Archie Hope of Balliol, the 17th Baronet, ... was up in North Berwick, where he lived, one Christmas vacation and he went to a Hunt Ball. He was bored absolutely sick by these old-timers going on and on. One he quoted as being really the most fantastically boring, was an old boy who kept haranguing him about the fishing customs of the hill tribes of the Brahmaputra. We thought that was quite absurd. The only way to cope with this was to start talking the same language back at such people, and so we founded this Club, based on the theme: "When I was in Poona ..."

This was the context for the Imperial Poona Yacht Club – it was a reaction against the Imperial bores of the day, and saw its role as making fun of them and their attitudes, using their language. As stated in the historical notes in the Club's handbook: "*It had been felt that a club embodying something of the Anglo-Indian culture was needed. The Club should regard Imperial Thinking as paramount.*"

The language is of those who are being mocked and is not to be taken seriously, but accepted for what it is – in modern parlance – a piss-take on the Imperial attitudes of the time.

If this is not understood, and the language taken seriously, the point will be missed.

Equally well, if the Imperial Poona Yacht Club ever takes itself seriously, it will have failed its founders.

THE FIRST INCARNATION

The Foundation

Somewhat surprisingly, for a Club which was set up on almost anti-establishment lines, a Minute Book was maintained up to the 1950s. It records:

The Imperial Poona Yacht Club was founded on Sunday, April 22nd, 1934 on the banks of the River Thames at Abingdon, the station of the Oxford University Yacht Club. During the Sunday afternoon's racing in which R.F.B. Bennett, then Vice Commodore of the O.U.Y.C., and A.W.A. Whitehead were taking part, there arrived Sir Archibald Hope, Baronet, and Charlie H. Johnston. They were expressing themselves in Anglo Indian terminology. These suggested the formation of a limited club on Anglo Indian lines, and there appeared to be three good reasons for its formation.

1. Experiences, of those present, with Anglo Indians, culminating perhaps in information given recently to Sir Archibald Hope on the subject of the Fishing Customs of the Hill Tribes of the Brahmaputra.

2. The need for an association to knit together the small but diffuse collection of people who had in recent years, in their various permutations and combinations, been at the back of much party-making.

3. The desirability of some society to collect keen young sailing men, often but not always from the Universities, without the rather unjustified premises on which the Oxford and Cambridge Sailing Society had been founded.

The Oxford & Cambridge Sailing Society had been formed on 24th February 1934, but Reggie Bennett had not been invited to be a member. On the face of it, this was surprising given that he had sailed for Oxford in the Varsity Match since 1931, and was the Vice Commodore (senior undergraduate) of the OUYC, but Reggie and Stewart Morris (the Society's leading light) never got on. Reggie may have been using Anglo Indian terminology to mock those returning from India, but he was also making fun of Stewart and his Society.

One can perhaps see some of Reggie's mischief-making in evidence in the report in the other history in this volume that *"the Society's founding meeting heard that 'certain people' from the Royal Corinthian Yacht Club* [where Reggie was known to sail] *considered it* [the Oxford & Cambridge Sailing Society] *a name to which the persons present had no claim – it would not be representative of either Oxford or Cambridge."*

Reggie uses rather similar language when referring to the Society's *"rather unjustified premises"*.

Given the largely similar nursery for the two organisations, it is interesting to note that, Henry Trefusis, a friend of Reggie's at school and Oxford, was the only founding member of both clubs.

Two of Poona's other early members were later elected to the Society – Richard Webster in 1936 and John Palmer in 1938, so membership of the two Clubs did overlap, but only very slightly in the initial years.

The Rules & Constitution

The four present, on the banks of the Thames, when the momentous decision to form the Club was made, proceeded that evening to formulate a constitution and draw up the Club's rules:

It was decided to found the Club on Poona, that name so dear to the Anglo Indian. And it was considered good that the Club should be a yacht club. The prefix 'Imperial' was chosen to avoid confusion with clubs which held a Royal warrant. The Club was therefore named the Imperial Poona Yacht Club.

It must have been a good evening, because the set of rules they produced have largely remained unaltered, and still provide amusement when one appreciates how firmly their tongues were placed in their cheeks.

Membership was limited to fifteen '*Pukkah Sahibs*', who had to be unmarried men. While the title of Commodore was traditional (although the holder is more usually referred to as The Commode), there were to be no Vice or Rear Commodores – instead they were the Great White Vice and Great Gorgeous Rear. All members were given appropriate Anglo Indian names.

The original rules and constitution read as follows:

IMPERIAL POONA YACHT CLUB
RULES AND CONSTITUTION

1. **The Club** shall be known as the Imperial Poona Yacht Club.
2. **The Objects of the Club** shall be
    (a) To promote Imperial Feeling.
    (b) To promote Team Sailing in Imperial Waters.
    (c) To promote Coloured Races among all Recognised Yacht Clubs within the British Empire.

3. **The Station of the Club**.
   The Club will have no particular station other than the British Empire.
4. **Politics**.
   The Club will be non-political, all members being pledged to an Imperial Party.
5. **Membership**.
   Membership shall be limited to 15, all of whom must be Pukka Sahibs, members of Recognised Yacht Clubs within the British Empire, and unmarried British Subjects. No memsahibs are eligible.
6. **Election to Membership**.
   A candidate for election must be vouched for in writing to the Secretariat-Wallah by no less than 4 (four) members to whom he is personally known. The Secretariat-Wallah shall then circularise all members, and if two black topees are received within a month the candidature will lapse. Otherwise the candidate shall be considered elected.
7. **Entrance Fee**.
   There shall be an entrance fee of 64 (sixty-four) sixty-fourths (64ths) of a rupee, payable on election to membership.
8. **Cessation of Membership**.
   Membership shall terminate automatically on
   (a) Marriage.
   (b) Death.
   (c) Ceasing to be a member of a Recognised Yacht Club within the British Empire.
   (d) Bankruptcy, unless otherwise authorised by the Club.
   (e) Temporarily, on imprisonment or deportation.
9. **Marriage**.
   Any member contracting a marriage shall stand a dinner to all the other members of the Club, who shall retaliate, if desired, with a guard of honour.
10. **Officers**.
    The Officers of the Club shall consist of: a Commodore, a Great White Vice, a Great Gorgeous Rear, a Secretariat-Wallah, a Finance Member, an Honorary Chaplain (who shall be the then Archbishop of Poona if the said Archbishop of Poona be a member of a Recognised Yacht Club within the British Empire, not legally married, etc., etc.), a serang, a crackswain, a shanty-muezzin, a donkeyman, a punkah-wallah, a currie-fellah, and any others that may hereafter be instituted.

11. **Committee**.
    The Committee shall consist of the officers together with the other members.
12. **Commodore**.
    The Commodore shall be chosen for his ability and experience in handling Coloured Races.
13. **Tiffin**.
    An annual Tiffin shall be held whenever circumstances require, and at it the toast of "Poona" shall always be drunk.
14. **Quorum**.
    Four or more members may constitute a Tiffin.
15. **Chair**.
    At Tiffin the senior officer present shall take the chair.
16. **Speeches**.
    At Tiffin every member present must make a speech.
17. **Bhoi**.
    If at Tiffin the Hon. Haro-Bhoi be present the Ceremonies of Foulin and Roundin the Bhoi shall be gone through.
18. **Class**.
    The Club shall sail for preference in the Brahmaputra Restricted or Swettipore One-Design Class (hereinafter referred to as the S.O.D.'s). Any class may be so designated for the time being, and failing this a class shall be constituted with not less than one design per boat.
19. **Motto**.
    The Motto of the Club shall be "Chota Hazri."
20. **Insignia**.
    The Club tie and Burgee may be obtainable at Messrs. W.H. Walker's, The Broad, Oxford.
21. **Finance**.
    A statement of accounts shall be issued by the Secretariat-Wallah or Finance Member or both.
22. **Alteration of Rules**.
    Any rule may be altered on notice to the Secretariat-Wallah and circularization by him, provided that 2/3 (two thirds) of the members agree to the proposed alteration.
23. **Resignation Forms**.
    Resignation forms may always be obtained from the Hon. Chaplain Sahib, provided that sufficient notice be given.

The Club's motto of "*Chota Hazri*", was once translated by Reggie as "*There is nothing worse than a continental breakfast*". According to Jyotsna Shahane on her website, thecookscottage, it actually refers to "*a little brekker of tea and biscuits, usually served in the bedroom, in a propah tea set dedicated to the purpose. This was followed somewhat later by a pukka larger breakfast."*

Initial Members & Inaugural Tiffin

The foundation members are recorded in the Minute Book as:

Sir Archibald Hope, Bt	Commodore
C.H. Johnston	Great White Vice
J.F.R. Mitchell	Great Gorgeous Rear
R.F.B. Bennett	Chaplain
A.W.A. Whitehead	Secretariat Wallah
J.H.M. Rabone	Punkah Wallah

With the following also elected immediately:

Henry Trefusis	Shanty-Muezzin
P.J. Norton	Ayah
T.C. Maples	Acting Haro-Bhoi
P.P. Powell	Haro-Bhoi & Donkeyman
J.C.L. Palmer	Serang

And the numbers bought up to the full fifteen the following month:

F.O.S Dobell	Irrigation Fellah
R.N. Webster	Untouchable
Squadron Leader W.A.K. Dalzell	Currie Fellah
Flight Officer G.K. Fairtlough	Djinn

Some of this membership reflects Reggie's other love at the time – flying, which was also the subject of an incident early on in the Club's history:

Shortly after the inception of the Club, the Commodore and Chaplain were submitted to an aerial attack by an Auro Lynx SO4N, containing F/O G.K. Fairtlough, RAF, and Mr P.C. Wheeler, OUAS. This aircraft then proceeded to traverse some telephone wires over the river, removing them en route. Justification was pleaded on the grounds that, in the course of many miles flown over many kinds of water in the Fleet Air Arm, the pilot had never encountered wire before.

Purportedly as a result of this incident, Fairtlough was "*posted away on the grounds of 'unsuitability (temperamental) for instructing undergraduates'.*"

However, as luck would have it, the Club's inaugural Tiffin coincided with this and so doubled up as his Farewell Tiffin, which was held at the Oxford University Air Squadron, Manor Road on 11th May 1934. Seven members were present and five other guests. Although not of very good quality, the photo of this very first Tiffin has to be included.

The Imperial Poona Yacht Club's First Tiffin, 11th May, 1934

There were multiple speeches, various performances, climbing of the flag posts and moving of vehicles. But the echoes of Brideshead Revisted are clear in the account of what happened to the unfortunate Philip Wheeler who was a guest (and probably still recovering from his earlier flight):

Mr Wheeler toured Oxford on an unlit bicycle, twice circulating the Clarendon Garage at high speed before being apprehended by a policeman standing 'like Christ crucified' in the gateway. He proceeded to mislead the policeman and made an unsuccessful attempt to escape. Being bailed out by the Proctors [University officials]*, his whole misdeeds were laid bare and he was, after an angry scene with the Dean of New College, sent down, the first Poona martyr.*

Probably as a result of this performance, he was elected a member in October 1934.

His election was possible because two members had left the Club. P.P. Powell was *"deported and made Hon. Canadian Representative. Later to be engaged to be married."* And J.H.M. Rabone was, more mysteriously, *"required to resign through non-fulfilment of conditions of membership."* (Apparently he had ceased to be a member of a recognised yacht club).

If individuals did not meet the Club's strict criteria (usually because they were married), but were felt to behave sufficiently imperially, they were elected to Honorary membership, as was the case for F.G. Mitchell (Honorary Colonel in Chief) and Colin Ratsey (Honorary Sails Manager).

Further Tiffins

The Minute Book records eleven further Tiffins which were held in 1934:

14th July	Royal Corinthian Yacht Club, Burnham
18th July	Officers' Mess, RAF Eastchurch, Kent
20th July	Officers' Mess, RAF Eastchurch, Kent
26th July	On board 'Eclipse' at Newhaven
28th July	On board 'Eclipse' at Cowes (this Tiffin *"continued for several days!"*)
1st – 8th September	During Burnham Week (*"throughout the week the toast of Poona was drunk"*).
10th October	The Aerodrome Hotel, Croydon
10th November	At Oxford, under the auspices of OUYC
22nd November	Royal Thames Yacht Club, Knightsbridge
24th November	Burnham-on-Crouch
30th November	101 Piccadilly and the Running Horse hostelry

These appear to have been a variety of informal events which took place whenever at least four members of the Club (as required by the Constitution) gathered together. While not strictly a flag officer of the Club, it was clear who was the driving force behind all of them – the only person present at all twelve Tiffins in 1934 – Reggie Bennett!

Sailing

But it would be wrong to suppose that Poona's only activity in its first year was at Tiffins.

Roy Mitchell and Reggie Bennett represented England in the Twelve Square Metre International Sharpie Class at Kiel. *"Against the most strenuous opposition from Germany, Holland and Switzerland, and* less strenuous from Sweden, Italy, Finland and Poland, the results showed England first with five wins and one second in six races."

At Cowes, five members of the Oxford University Varsity Match team were Poona members, and the sixth (David Wilson) was subsequently elected. Unfortunately they failed to achieve victory over the Tabs, and a draw was declared.

In America, Roy Mitchell and Colin Ratsey represented the Club on board 'Endeavour' challenging for the Americas Cup. Meanwhile, in the UK, Reggie and John Palmer sailed on board another J Class yacht, 'Shamrock V', for a month, with a record of "*4 (or 5) firsts and 7 seconds in 16 races.*"

Insignia

The Club's tie was designed to be worn with Morning Dress by the guard of honour when a member resigned through matrimony, and had already been used for such a purpose within six months of the foundation of the Club. It had a silver-grey background, with red topees.

The burgee similarly had a red topee, but this time on a yellow background. (The famous red balls were only introduced after the War).

Gillie Potter also designed a yachting cap badge for the Club during Burnham Week, some of which are still in the ownership of Poona members. The original sketch is shown overleaf.

The Following Years

Nine Tiffins were held in 1935 in a variety of venues, with Reggie again being the most regular attendee.

The weekend of 2nd and 3rd March saw a Tiffin in Oxford on the Saturday with ten attendees, which, since there were fourteen members at the time, was deemed to be a record – 71% attendance. This achievement prompted another Tiffin to be celebrated the following day, which was also the first recorded visit by the Club to two hostelries it would come to know well – firstly The Perch at Binsey, and then onto The Trout at Godstow.

The first overseas Tiffin (and the Club's twenty first) was also held in this year (1935), when Reggie Bennett, Archie Hope, Colin Ratsey and his wife went to America to compete in the Frostbite Gold Cup in Larchmont. While not strictly quorate, with only three members present, it was still deemed a Tiffin and resulted in the Club's first publicity in America:

The voyage to America of the Commodore and Chaplain proved itself such a hurrah-party for Poona that the Hon. Sails Manager and manageress must be considered, with them, to have formed a quorum. The New York Herald Tribune (Bill Taylor) wrote about the Club and its racing flag. And the joke went down quite absurdly well. Walter Rowe supplied us with topees and we elected him our Mother Superior (honorary).

There was quite a break after this encounter, which was partly caused by the run up to the Olympics in 1936. Colin Ratsey and Reggie Bennett were runners-up in the trials for the Star Class and selected as reserves.

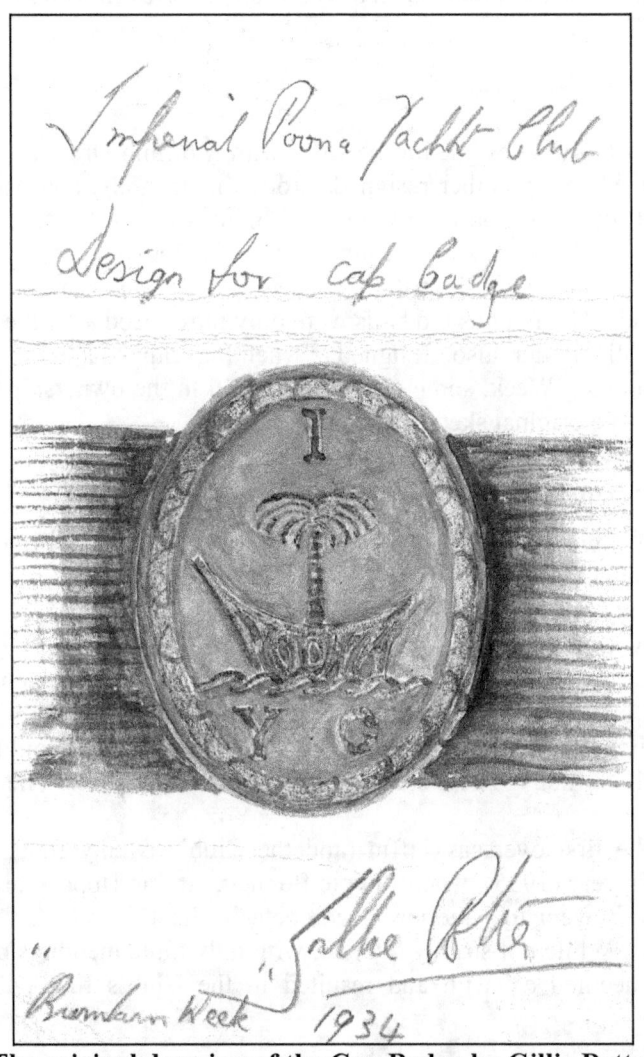

The original drawing of the Cap Badge by Gillie Potter

The Denouement

Only six Tiffins were held in 1936 and none in 1937. It seems that Reggie's time was now filled with other things.

In February 1937, he passed his medical qualifications, and was soon working as a locum around the country. He also contested the London County Council elections in East Woolwich, joined the Royal Naval Volunteer Reserve (RNVR), and was a special constable in the Metropolitan River Police at Wapping, as well as sailing and flying as often as he could.

He spent the following winter in India as pilot to the Maharajah of Rajpipla, and spoke warmly of his time there.

On his return, in 1938, he realised that the Imperial Poona Yacht Club was no longer quorate, as he explained in his memoir:

It [the Imperial Poona Yacht Club] *had a rule which established a quorum* [four] *for any meeting, and another condition was that bachelordom was obligatory. So, as the undergraduates of yesteryear fell away into the arms of matrimony, our numbers had fallen rapidly until just before the war broke out our club had to be dissolved. It was dissolved in the Resident Clerk's room, or Resident Secretary's room, in the Foreign Office, where Charlie Johnston, the Vice Commodore, was then serving. The three remaining bachelors and the fourth, the last backslider, had solemnly toasted the Club and called it off.*

Present on this auspicious occasion, the Club's twenty eigth Tiffin, was Charlie Johnston (Great White Vice), Reggie Bennett (Chaplain), Richard Fairey and Tim Bennett (Reggie's brother).

The Minute Book records the Club being formally dissolved *"as its purpose had been achieved."*

And so, a Club started on the banks of the Thames was dissolved at the Foreign Office after a brief existence of what appears to have been two active and two inactive years.

The historical notes in the Club's handbook record: *"war followed, though not immediately"*.

THE SECOND INCARNATION

The Reformation

The Second World War saw three Poona members lose their lives: Tim Bennett, Philip Wheeler and Arthur Whitehead, and, according to the Minute Book *"the original membership was otherwise altogether scattered."* The record continues:

In 1946, when peace had broken out again, strong hints were given, from both Burnham and Cowes, that the Culture of Poona was once more sadly needed in the world.

The Club was therefore re-formed by five of the original members – Reggie Bennett, Peter Norton, Constable Roberts, Tiny Mitchell and Frank Spriggs – together with eight newly co-opted members, making thirteen members in all.

The first official Tiffin of the new era was at Hamble on Sunday 28th July 1946 during a match against the Centreboard Racing Club, which Poona won. Cowes Week followed shortly afterwards and all the members bar one (who had been deported to the British Embassy in Brazil) attended.

Democracy, of a sort, arrived at Poona in the winter of 1946, when the thirteen members were invited to propose candidates for the two vacancies and vote for the Flag Officers. Reggie Bennett was duly elected as Commodore, with Sir Heneage Ogilvie as Great White Vice and Steve Longsdon as Great Gorgeous Rear, although the latter's election was only possible because the rule of disqualification from membership for visiting Poona was waived!

Coupled with this election, the original Great White Vice, Charles Johnston, returned from diplomatic missions in Japan and Egypt and re-joined the Club, and John Carew-Jones was also elected – filling the fifteen places available.

As a joke, the Club applied for recognition by the YRA (predecessor to the current RYA) and were rather surprised that some took them more seriously than they took themselves. The Club's name duly appeared both on the list of YRA recognised clubs and the Lloyd's list.

The Redefinition

Six sahibs and six memsahibs (including a Miss Henrietta Crane, making her first appearance in our history) gathered in the Royal Thames Yacht

Club in Knightsbridge on Thursday 19th December 1946 to review the Rules and Constitution and made the following changes:
- The bachelordom rule was removed.
- The disqualification of anyone visiting Poona was amended to require that *"any officer or member who completes a pilgrimage to Poona assumes the style and title of 'hadji' and shall dye his beard blue."*
- The flag of the club was changed to the now customary yellow with three red balls.

Following its own recognition by the YRA, the Club decided to reverse its earlier policy and formally recognised the Yacht Racing Association. This process has continued as it has subsequently recognised the Yachting Association and then the Royal Yachting Association. The Club is committed to a policy of continuing this process as required.

For the first time, an annual subscription of one guinea was imposed, but members who were shocked by such a financial imposition were left in a difficult position: *"Members who feel unable or unwilling to contribute are requested to send in their resignations to the Secretariat Wallah. These resignations will be refused and a fine of two guineas imposed forthwith"*!

However, despite much chasing, three members had failed to pay their subscription some two years later, and they were therefore deemed to have resigned.

But it was not just the members who were having difficulties with the idea of the Club having money. Lloyds Bank were unhappy with the idea of an account being held by a Club in which all its members constituted the committee. To pacify them, a smaller committee had to be established as far as the bank was concerned.

The full membership limit of fifteen was somewhat being ignored at this time, with at least four new members being elected in late 1946 and two old members (Richard Webster and John Palmer) re-joining. At a Tiffin at the Royal Thames Yacht Club in February 1947, the membership was formally increased from fifteen to twenty five, where it remains to this day.

The twenty fifth member was elected a few months later, and a waiting list was established. In order to reduce this, it was decided that any member who had been out of the United Kingdom for twelve consecutive months would be treated as deported and taken off the active list to allow some on the waiting list into membership.

As this waiting list grew, more stringent measures were required, and in 1949 a rule was added that cessation of membership could happen *"temporarily, on imprisonment (whether civil, service or domestic) and deportation."* As a result, two members ceased to be on the active list for reasons of deportation, two for service imprisonment and one for domestic imprisonment.

Later that year it was also decided that membership would also cease on *"ceasing to think Imperially."*

On New Year's Day 1950, the active list of members numbered twenty four. In addition there were two on the Deported list, two Honorary members and nine on the waiting list, although it would appear that only one of these ever made it to Active membership.

Tiffins

The Club certainly had a new lease of life, with four Tiffins recorded in the first two months of 1947, and many more throughout the year.

One (with the required four members present) was even held during the Oxford & Cambridge Sailing Society's match against the Dragon Class (Solent Division), indicating that membership of both clubs was no longer frowned upon.

Other Tiffins in 1947 took place on the Clyde and at Cowes and Burnham as members got to grips with the first real season's sailing since the war.

Perhaps the largest gathering of members took place on 27th November 1947, when twelve members and five guests gathered in the Cock Tavern in Fleet Street to mark the last bachelor night of the Commodore and Chaplain, Reggie Bennett.

This was followed, the next day, by the Club's first Durbar – to celebrate the marriage of Reggie and Henrietta. It is recorded: *"This was an orderly affair, whether it was due to the occasion or whether from the night before, it is hard to say."*

At the next Tiffin a tighter definition of the Club's gatherings was agreed:
- Chota Hazri – up to six members
- Tiffin – seven members and over
- Durbar – full membership

Occasionally Tiffins were made more public, as in February 1949 when a journalist from the Evening Standard *"accidentally attended"* part of one and wrote about it in the 'In London Last Night' section of the paper.

Another large gathering of the Club occurred when fifteen active and two honorary members were present at the Island Sailing Club's Jubilee Dinner and Dance celebrating that Club's 60th anniversary at the Dorchester Hotel in March 1949.

Reggie Bennett's Stag Night, 27th November, 1947

	John Palmer	Jack Dewsberry	Cecil Knight		James Tilney
Joe Brunton	Ernest Harston	Bruce Kinnier-Wilson	Jack Longsdon		Steve Longsdon
					Reggie Bennett
	John Dunn	Tony Tollemache	John Mead		Frank Spriggs
					Peter Norton
	Slim Behenna	Jack Raymond	Mike Crean		

A landmark Chota Hazri (with five members present) took place in January 1950 for the first and only unholy alliance in marriage between two Poona offspring when Douglas Howden Hume (son of James Howden Hume, Honorary Pipah) married June Spriggs (daughter of Sir Frank Spencer Spriggs, Kitehawk).

Tiffins continued apace in 1950 with eight recorded at various sailing clubs and other hostelries around the country.

Sailing

Matches against other clubs were revived in 1949, with a win against Lee-on-Solent SC and losses recorded against the Oxford University YC and Hamble River SC. The latter match attracted quite a bit of press attention because Reggie Bennett was standing for parliament as the Conservative candidate for Gosport and Fareham.

It is interesting to think that in 1949, tales of the Imperial Poona Yacht Club, and its irreverent ways, were felt to be a positive story for a prospective parliamentary candidate and press releases were issued – I suspect the same would not be true in today's "politically correct" environment!

Nevertheless, the match was reported in the Evening Standard, Southern Daily Echo, Hampshire Telegraph & Post and one other unidentifiable newspaper.

Reggie was duly elected with a *"vast majority"* in 1950. One of his first steps was to help create the House of Commons Yacht Club, of which he was appointed as Secretary. The Minute Book records: *"A number of messages were received congratulating him on his first step towards high parliamentary office."*

The House of Commons YC made its first appearance in public in a three cornered match between themselves, Lee-on-Solent SC and the Imperial Poona YC at Lee-on-Solent on 23rd July 1950. Unfortunately an onshore gale was blowing and the boats could not be launched, so sailing was cancelled. Instead *"a programme of sporting contests"* was organised by Charles Taylor, MP for Eastbourne.

As part of this, a beer drinking race was run, with a team, largely composed of House of Commons YC members, beating a Poona / Lee-on-Solent team. The event was photographed and witnessed by Sir Charles MacAndrew, Deputy Speaker of the House of Commons (and Commodore of the House of Commons YC). Again, something that might not happen (or certainly not be publicly photographed) today, but recorded here to show that politicians did not always take themselves as seriously as they do now.

An attempt to hold this fixture was repeated on 24th September 1950, but this was again unsuccessful.

The match was finally held in the summer of 1951 and reported, with photographs in an unidentified publication, but possibly Country Life. Lee-on-Solent won, Poona was second and the House of Commons bought up the rear.

Poona and the House of Commons YC competed in another three way match, this time against the United Hospitals SC at Burnham on Crouch in 1951. This again resulted in victory for the home team, with

Poona second and the House of Commons third.

Beer Drinking Race Involving The House of Commons YC, Imperial Poona YC and Lee-on-Solent SC, 23rd July, 1950

Winning Team (front to back)
Tufton Beamish, HoCYC
Michael Crean, IPYC
Stephens, HoCYC
Terry Clarke, HoCYC
Charles Taylor, HoCYC
Reggie Bennett, HoCYC, IPYC

Losing Team (front to back)
Joe Hannen, LoSSC, IPYC
Eric Hannen, LoSSC
Gerald Hume Wright, LoSSC
V J van der Byl, LoSSC
James Talbot, IPYC
Hugh Somerville, IPYC
John Chamier, IPYC

The 58th Tiffin

Reggie's election to the House of Commons also provided the opportunity for the Club which mocked the establishment to meet at the heart of it when the 58th Tiffin was held at the House of Commons on Monday 6th November 1950.

It was a working dinner for Reggie as proceedings were interrupted when *"the Commodore withdrew to record his vote at his place of work"*!

Items on the agenda included:

- Defacing our Ensign – rejected on the grounds that it was *"either below or above the Club's dignity."*
- The need for a Sacred Cow – inconclusive.
- A suggestion that one Tiffin a year be for men only – agreed, but changed to *"members only"*.
- Registering disgust that the health of the King Emperor is no longer drunk in the Indian Army – withdrawn on the basis that *"it was virtually impossible to drink anyone's health in India owing to the prohibition."*

The Evening Standard announced the event, but it was an unnamed Irish paper which went to town about it:

> **Egad, Sir! These Imperial Pooners Take Some Beating**
> *In the British House of Commons last Monday, there was a smashing "do". Twenty-five pukka-pukka sahibs sat down together to have what we might call dinner, but which they elect to call Tiffin. They were members of the Imperial Poona Yacht Club – probably one of the most outrageous sports bodies in the world.*
>
> *There are sports bodies which are snobbish ... there are bodies which are very snobbish ... but Imperial Poona Yacht Club takes the biscuit. No doubt they have the usual qualifications for an exclusive club, but they have one in addition which we can appreciate fully here and fairly beats Banagher.*
>
> *They lay down that any man who knows one word of Hindustani (language spoken in Poona) is not eligible for membership, and if, as a member, he learns one word, he has his gold braid and buttons cut off and is drummed out.*
>
> *I don't believe that, even in its palmist days, the Kildare Street Club would have gone as far as that, even though their views of the Irish language may have been severe.*
>
> *One can easily imagine the "Imperial Pooners" going about their business with corks in their ears lest they hear words of Hindustani. No doubt they have a Vigilance Committee with their ears cocked waiting for that one word which would mean expulsion. Incidentally, they limit their membership to 25 – but I doubt if there is any need for a limit with such a regulation.*

OVERSEAS EXPANSION

By the early 1950s, Poona was firmly re-established in the UK, with regular Tiffins, Chota Hazris and sailing matches. Once the home of the UK government had been invaded in November 1950, thought turned to extending Poona's empire.

Revolting Colonies

In December 1950, there was a meeting specifically called to discuss a crisis over ties – the number ordered from the manufacturer greatly exceeded the number bought by members, and the manufacturer was chasing payment.

At the meeting: *"The Commodore produced photographic evidence that our American Honorary Members were 'thinking Imperially' and it was decided to try to unload the surplus tie stock upon them at a suitably inflated price."*

How these small things shape the course of history. A concern over tea saw the Americans begin to separate from the United Kingdom, but now a crisis over ties saw some strengthening of the bond between Imperial Thinkers on both sides of the Atlantic!

When the US Six Metre team, led by Robert Meyer, came to race against the UK in 1951 there was a meeting with *"the members of the Imperial Poona YC 'Lodge' in the Revolting Colonies ... much business was done including the sale of 15 ties at exorbitant price and the scrutinising of their charter."*

A few days later *"at a simple, though moving, ceremony in London"* on 26th July, 1951, the charter was duly consecrated and signed by Reggie Bennett and Robert Meyer.

As soon as the Revolting Colonies Outpost had been established, and before they had time to regroup on their native soil, a sailing match was held between them and the home station of the Imperial Poona Yacht Club in Cowes. This was held in centre-board sailing dinghies and the Revolting Colonies won.

Three years earlier, Reggie had spotted an old quart beer mug standing on the floor of a Cowes grocer's shop, catching the tap drippings from a barrel of vinegar. With Mr Biddlecomes's consent, he exchanged it for a jam jar.

He titled this the Thunder Mug and presented it to the victors, who proudly took the mug back to Long Island and had it cleaned, mounted and inscribed. It now became a permanent challenge trophy to be competed for whenever the two arms of the Club got together.

CHARTER OF A WESTERN HEMISPHERE STATION
of the
IMPERIAL POONA YACHT CLUB

NAME	The REVOLTING COLONIES OUTPOST of the IMPERIAL POONA YACHT CLUB.
STATION	Revolting Colonies Unlimited and the Island of Yap.
MEMBERS	Twelve and one half Members, all of whom have read "SUBMERSION IS THE BETTER PART OF VALOR" at the Union Inn, Cowes, Isle of Wightistan, UK, or have pursued same philosophy in Imperial waters for a protracted period, except that whenever a Member re-enters the Station of the IMPERIAL POONA YACHT CLUB a vacancy shall be deemed to exist in the membership of the REVOLTING COLONIES OUTPOST Station which may be filled provided that the total membership never exceeds twenty-five Members. No memsahibs are eligible.
SUB-MOTTO	"LET US BE REVOLTING" to be executed in Latin and Indian by the Revolting Charge of Intimate Imperial Home Relations.
OFFICERS	The Officers of the Station shall consist of: The RCO Commodore, the RCO Great White Vice, the RCC Great Gorgeous Rear, the RCO Secretariat-Wallah, the RCO Finance Member, an Honorary Chaplain, the Secretariat-Wallah of the Recently-Impressed Late-Deported, the Revolting Charge of Intimate Imperial Home Relations, the RCO Serang, the RCO Djinn-Krooboy, The RCO Donkeyman, the RCO Punkah-Wallah, the RCO Shanty-Muezzin, the RCO Currie-Fellah, and any others that may hereafter be instituted.
TIFFIN	A bi-annual Tiffin shall be held whenever circumstances require during the Monsoon season, and a bi-annual Tiffin shall be held whenever circumstances require during the Dry season, and at Tiffin the toast of "Poona" shall always be drunk and shall always be followed by the toast of "Let us be revolting."
ET ALIA	The Rules and Constitution of the Imperial Poona Yacht Club shall govern in cases of doubt.
AUTHORITY	LETTER DATED 26 July 1951 from Commodore Dr. Reginald Bennett, VRD, MP.

After The Signing Of The Revolting Colonies Charter, 26th July, 1951

Back row: Jack Maclay, Trevor de Hamel, Buddy Bombard, Sir Heneage Ogilvie, Alan Priddy, Wilson Cross, Stan Priddy, John Morgan, John Palmer, Glen Foster, Peter Macdonald
Front row: Charles Taylor, Magnus Konow, Charlie MacAndrew, Robert Meyer Jr., Osborne Dobell, Reggie Bennett, Robert Meyer Sr.

A newspaper report of this first match between the two teams concludes:

In the contest there is but one rule governing the competition craft. It is that the competition is limited to sailboats 'having no more than one design each', a joke which will appeal to racing yachtsmen.
  The Imperial Poona Yacht Club was born among undergraduates at Oxford in 1931 [actually 1934]. *Dr Bennett was among those who started it as a satirical, but good humoured, comment on the social importance attached, by some military men of those days, to service in Poona. The reason for it has gone, but the spirit and comradeship have survived.*

After all this activity in 1951, 1952 appears to have been a quiet year, with just one event recorded – the annual match against the Oxford University

YC. Those who know how this match developed in later years may be surprised to know that the racing was conventional, with no strange rules.

The rules used later actually originated in North America when, during the Autumn of 1953, Reggie Bennett and other Poona members were there for the races against America in the Six metre class. Once again, the original Imperial Poona Yacht Club competed against the Revolting Colonies for the Thunder Mug.

This was reported in the Times, on 30th September, by a 'special correspondent' – special in that he was the IPYC's Commode, Reggie Bennett. The report is reprinted here by kind permission of Times Newspapers.

THE THUNDER MUG

BRITISH YACHTSMEN BRING IT HOME
FROM OUR SPECIAL CORRESPONDENT
OYSTER BAY, SEPT. 28

Yesterday morning, after a month's season of international racing in the six-metre class, a team race in centre board boats was organized. This was for the Thunder Mug, that battered old pewter quart pot that once did menial service in Cowes and now stands engraved on a plinth here – though not for long.

The class sailed for the purpose was the Ravens. These are large, powerful, half-deckers, 24ft. long, carrying a 200lb. centreplate. Ravens are exceedingly fast – they usually catch up six-metres – and they plane readily up to 12-15 knots. Their owners and crews are understandably enthusiastic and, to other less active yachtsmen, are generally known as "Raven maniacs". The winner and runner-up of the national Raven championships in Ohio earlier this month, J. Roosevelt's Old Crow and H. Anderson's Sleipnir, were in yesterday's event and the racing was keen.

The course was from the club pontoon, about half a mile to windward, through the anchorage, to the great schooner Guinevere, twice round this ship in either direction, then a reach to a small seaplane moored near the beach off Centre Island, then back to the club pontoon, the finishing line to be crossed stern first. A nice south-west breeze was blowing.

Soon after the third gun the race officer, D. Jewett, announced the start, and the boats feverishly cast off and pushed one another off. In the melee J. Harrison was left, but made a very fast tack along the face of the pontoon while the rest were making their way through the anchored six-metre class. The rule that port tack had right of way produced many interesting situations, as did the various encounters while rounding

Guinevere. E. Ridder, in Gizmo, did great things in assisting his colleagues, and the seaplane turning-point was passed without any disqualifications. Of course, the final sternboard through the line was most spectacular. Gizmo assisting the commodore's boat astern to such good effect that the race was awarded on corrected times to the Imperial Poona Yacht Club, protests received, and copiously attested, not having been upheld.

The Thunder Mug thus returns to Great Britain, the only trophy to do so during the great sailing season here that is now drawing to a close. It is good that we do not return empty-handed, and we can assure our American hosts that we shall go back with our hearts full of their kindness and sportsmanship, awaiting eagerly our chance to entertain them in our waters in 1955.

Repulsive, But Not Revolting, Colonies

On 22nd April 1955, exactly twenty one years after the Imperial Poona Yacht Club was founded, the Club established its second overseas outpost – the Repulsive But Non-Revolting Canadian Outpost at Toronto.

The Repulsive, But Not Revolting, Colonists During A Sail Past In 1962

However, this international expansion caused problems with the monetary basis of the Club. Bill Gooderham, the Repulsive Commodore wrote:

Regarding annual fees and entrance fees: the Constitution is set up for payment in rupees; as they are very scarce in the locality of our outpost could we use some other type of wampum [the North American Indian currency], *that being anything which might be barter-able . We would suggest an ounce of uranium, rum, or something else that is easier to obtain than rupees.*

The Reactionary Colonies

The third Poona outpost was in Bermuda and called the Reactionary Colonies. The Club's handbook states that this was "*duly founded on a date now lost in the mists of history*", and the first documentary evidence of it is from the mid 1960s, but it was clearly up and running before then, although not before 1957.

The outpost's own charter and constitution (dated 1986) is no more informative, stating:

Whereas, on a date which is lost to the memory of man, but generally taken to be the 22nd day of April in One Thousand Nine Hundred and something (being the anniversary of the date on which The Great Philanthropic and Benevolent Institution known as the Imperial Poona Yacht Club was founded) a group of like-minded and Imperially-thinking Pukka Sahibs caused a Bermuda Outpost of the said Imperial Poona Yacht Club to be established in Hamilton in the Colony of Bermuda known as the "Reactionary Colonists' Outpost" or the "Reactionary Onions".

They too revolted against the traditional currency of the rupee, and, instead, used Bermuda Pearl Onions (Gin soaked).

As well as having backwards races like that held in America in 1953, the Bermuda outpost introduced the backwards Tiffin, starting with the cigars and brandy and working their way towards the soup.

DEVELOPMENTS AT HOME

Meanwhile the 1950s saw the British home station of the Imperial Poona Yacht Club flourish, and an influx of new blood.

The Club maintained its limit of twenty five active members, with candidates mostly, but not exclusively, proposed by Reggie Bennett and then submitted to the membership for approval. Generally prospective members were good sailors who shared Reggie's sense of fun, a number being graduates from the Oxford University Yacht Club, although this was certainly not the only source of members.

Uffa Fox

Reggie first met Uffa Fox (the renowned boat designer, sailor and character) in 1929 when he sailed his dinghy across to the Isle of Wight while still at Winchester College. He happened to walk past someone working on an upturned 14 ft dinghy and asked him where he could get fresh water and whether he knew a person called Uffa Fox who lived round there. It was Uffa himself, working on the celebrated 'Avenger'. This started a lifelong association between the two characters which Reggie recalls was *"attended by many a remarkable event, always amusing."*

One such event was when Uffa revived the playing of cricket on the Brambles sand bank in the Solent on 15th September 1954. Uffa captained a Yachtsmen of Cowes team against Parkhurst Prison. As the tide went out, Reggie and Mike Parker planted the Imperial Poona burgee in the sand and the game proceeded until the sands began to be covered again. Near the end, the Governor of Parkhurst Prison vanished under water suddenly when running backwards for a high catch. The Times reported the match saying *"no doubt the venue was chosen with a view to preventing the escape of any of the players"*!

Uffa was elected to the Club in 1955 and Time Magazine also recorded the presence of both Uffa and the Imperial Poona Yacht Club at Cowes Week in that year in an article entitled *'Renaissance Man'*. This article talked about Uffa donning a pith helmet and leading the Imperial Poona Yacht Club in song. The article can be found by typing "Imperial Poona Yacht Club" into Google, but sadly the rights to reproduce even a paragraph of it here were prohibitively expensive.

Cricket On The Brambles, 15th September, 1954 The Yachtsmen Of Cowes Against Parkhurst Prison

Backward Races

While we have reported on matches against Oxford, these had taken the form of conventional team races, but, following the innovations seen in the race for the Thunder Mug in America in 1953, the rules changed somewhat.

In 1955, a rule was introduced into the IPYC constitution that *"An annual race shall be held from time to time in the cradle of the Backward Races."* The cradle of the Backward Races is, of course, Oxford and there were three simple rules for these races:

1. On the windward leg, port tack has right of way.
2. On reaching a mark, the mark has got to be hit. Rounding it without hitting it is not valid.
3. The downwind leg must be sailed backwards.

These reverse the standard rules of sailing where starboard tack has right of way, and marks must be rounded, but not touched. There is nothing in the usual rules to say which direction any leg has to be sailed, but backwards is certainly not the conventional, fastest or easiest approach. However, with practise, it is not only possible to sail effectively downwind backwards, but also to get a dinghy to plane in this manner!

The races traditionally took place in early November, partly to tie in with the celebrations at this time associated with the *"only person who has entered Parliament honestly"* (as MP Reggie described him), but it had the added advantage that it coincided with the International Yacht Racing Union's annual meetings which were held in London. This enabled some members of the Club's Outposts, who were in England for the meetings, to attend.

The best account of the match is provided by the then Secretariat-Wallah (later Commode) of the Revolting Colonies Outpost, Harry Anderson, reporting back to his members on the strange happenings on the banks of the Thames. Harry Anderson attended several of these matches over the years, even once when he was Chairman of the New York Yacht Club's America's Cup Committee which was facing a challenge from the UK. He described the 1965 match in the form of a play, and has kindly given permission for this to be reproduced here. (This was also featured in the American Sailor magazine in their April 1992 edition, which was a special "Fun Racing Issue". They added two cartoons by Scott Getchell which are reproduced here with the kind permission of the US Sailing Association).

ACT I

Scene 1. *Main room and bar of the pub 'The Perch' set back from the west bank of the Thames upstream from the Medley weir.*

In rain which is characterized locally as 'a bit of a spill' we skirt the sentinel – a boxer as uncommunicative as he is unflinching – and enter the pub to be greeted by Commodore Bennett decked in houndstooth.

The enthusiasm with which the members of the Home Station and their memsahibs and sub-memsahibs greet the R.C.O. [Revolting Colonies Outpost] envoy is reciprocated and quickly leads to thirst-slaking.

The Perch, already bulging with a medley of Poona members from the Active List and graduate and undergraduate members of the Oxford University Yacht Club so that the majority are perforce on their feet with heads bowed in the act either of quaffing another draught of bitters or of avoiding contact with one of the central ceiling rafters, is soon reinforced by those 'regulars' who dare brave the assemblage and by occasional fishermen seeking refuge from the weather.

It should be interposed that the 'Home Station' of the Poona, even more so than that of the R.C.O., takes an active interest in yachting among the University Clubs and enjoys a long tradition of replenishing its ranks from among graduates of the Oxford University Yacht Club. Oxford being the 'Cradle of The Backward Races', the annual regatta is quite appropriately conducted under their auspices.

Scene 2:   Dining room & side bar of the pub 'The Perch'.
Time: Wine and luncheon.

Although almost forty strong, twice the number for which arrangements have been made, Proprietor Chitty jovially and resourcefully meets the exigencies in the best tradition, and all hands, having attained a state of well-being in inverse ratio to the conditions prevailing outside, commence devouring a succulent deep-dish pie washed down with the finest Rhenish. Most colourful are the vestments ranging from the IPYC Commodore's

Sherlock Holmes ensemble, the Oxford UYC Vice Commodore's red and white striped shirt and every variety of the International Finn Class President, Vernon Stratton's, self-rescuing jackets worn by those who decline to rely on tweeds-against-the-Thames.

Scene 3:   Same as Scene 2
Time: Port after luncheon.

As luncheon pales, the port is poured, but inasmuch as a matter of serious business is raised from the floor, so a concomitant hue and cry is raised for more port to sustain the proceedings. Proprietor Chitty thereupon ransacks for sack and Commodore Bennett calls for a semblance of order. Same is gradually achieved, and the matter is put before the house regarding the sad state of morality among the members of the R.C.O. resulting in the resignation in the preceding decade of Honorary Chaplain, Commander C. Sherman Hoyt, under Rule 9 (a) [the rule requiring membership to cease on death]. *The four I.P.Y.C. members present who had completed pilgrimages to the shores of Oyster Bay in the R.C.O. home territory cite the uplifting effect which they experienced under the exhilarating influence of R.C.O. member 'Have-A-Scoop', Morgan S.A. Reichner, at which point in the proceedings, there being none contrary minded, there arises such a deafening clamor of approbation (we note that coincidentally the Proprietor is espied arriving with the aforementioned reinforcements of sack so it is not too clear whether developments serious or savory spark the clamor) that the Commodore hastens to declare his appointment as R.C.O. Chaplain duly confirmed.*

At this juncture one member of the gathering unwittingly unlatches a window against which another member is propped (space is somewhat at a premium today in The Perch, hence this precarious one), and the latter is bouleversed to the terrace. On recovering his aplomb he declares a slight diminution in the prevailing effluvium, and all hands proceed forthwith to the river bank.

ACT II

Scene 1:   On the west bank of the southwest elbow of the Thames above the bend above the Medley Weir Bridge. A sparse scattering of trees and bushes line the bank and extend inland bifurcating the grasslands tangentially to the bank. At a small dock, nine Alphas (akin to Fireflies but built of fibreglass) are secured.

The Race Officer takes his station under an umbrella with whistle and a quiver of two dozen rockets – the starting signal being the eleventh rocket to flare. It is never quite clear what point on the east bank constitutes the other end of the line, although as the contest evolves the question becomes more and more academic. Distributed up and downstream along the west bank are single fishermen seated beneath black or green umbrellas (the choice of colour presumably depending on their personal piscatorial predilections), but by mid-afternoon all gradually beat a retreat to escape from the inclement weather.

The east bank comprises a vast meadow (whence the appellation 'Port Meadow') stretching to the outskirts of Oxford whose spires and towers are visible in the distance. Stray cows graze the meadow and at the edge of the bank several score of geese are crouched ready to slip into the river and surround an unsuspecting Alpha.

I.P.Y.C. members, perhaps because of their advanced stage of edification, are not scheduled to participate on the first few races. The system of rocket starts seems to be working reasonably well, umbrellas work only with partial success and the underfooting is gradually deteriorating. It becomes increasingly difficult to sort out the O.U.Y.C. fleet from the fleet of the Medley Sailing Club whose downstream mark is farther downstream than, and whose upstream mark is farther upstream than, the respective rounding marks of the O.U.Y.C.

Scene 2:   Same place
Time: Late afternoon
At a suitable interval before dusk Poona enters the lists and the Secretariat-Wallah of the R.C.O. in towncoat and Homburg takes the helm with Yeti, Brian Appleton, as fore-deck man and connoisseur. Port tack has right of way which, since all yachts have to sail the leeward legs going backwards, contributes towards clearing up any possible confusion in the minds of the helmsmen of the Medley Sailing Club yachts, inasmuch as a port tack yacht sailing backwards is, for the purpose of another yacht sailing forward, ipso facto on the starboard tack close-hauled (since with the mainboom being held into the wind two-blocked to the shrouds there is no way to sail any closer to the wind with main filled).

After thirteen rockets a re-assemblage, or general recall of sorts, relegates the R.C.O. entry from the vanguard to the ruck. However, a third crew member in the form of Brian Appleton's fiancée, Susan, is plucked from the bank. Thus reinforced, the R.C.O. entry manoeuvres through a maze of what could best be described as the shambles of the once proud fleets of Poona and Oxford. R.C.O. is first yacht to 'bump' (rounding the marks being a method of yacht racing fit only for infidels and serving to create insoluble problems under the archaic, Beowulfian body of lore colloquially referred to in London as the 'I.Y.R.U. Racing Rules') the weather mark and to commence the retrograde movement upstream sailing backwards. Sowar ke Batcha, Noel Dobbs, is observed abandoning a sinking Alpha and swimming to shore, one arm aloft in an attempt to keep his timepiece dry – almost as futile a gesture under the circumstances as attempting to keep his codpiece dry. Simultaneously three Alphas become engaged in such a manner that all three capsize, the mast and rig of the weather yacht emerging clear and to leeward of the leeward-most yacht – clearly an instance of the weather yacht luffing two yachts overlapped to leeward and cause, therefore, only for 'Imperial' censure under the doctrine 'de minimis non curat lex'.

    Several of the crew members take to the river and proceed to attempt to right the above-mentioned sunken yacht which is now bow deep in the mud (it being the practice of backward races to use the bow tank covers to entrap the halyard tails, thereby creating an aperture and violating their watertight integrity). The stern tank, however, remains dry which, considering the fact that the transom is pointed majestically skyward, demonstrates that the Alpha is almost as aerodynamically sound in still flight as the Poona Swettipore One Designs.

    By now the melange of Alphas capsized, Medley Sailing Club craft circumnavigating the same, O.U.Y.C. Vice Commodore Tony Lunch porposing about amidst the cackle of geese (having followed the sage advice of WW1 submarine motto over the bar at the Union Inn at Cowes to the effect that 'Submersion is the better part of Valor') are becoming indistinguishable in the miasma of deepening dusk prompting the R.C. Officer to empty his quiver of the final cluster of rockets and call a halt to the proceedings.

Scene 3:   Denouement – downstream above the Medley Weir Bridge
The flotilla limps upwind, downstream, recovering the R.C.O.'s Homburg which is floating ahead and all yachts are beached for the night.

ACT III

Scene 1:   In Oxford proper at the headquarters of the Oxford University Yacht Club – Committee Room.
Time: Low Tea.

By various conveyances and stages, contestants and spectators assemble at the honorary and ancient headquarters of the O.U.Y.C. and partake of tea, switch to dry vestments and await the summations of the scorekeepers. At this juncture the final business of the meeting is transacted, namely that it be the mission of the I.P.Y.C. to construct a scoring system for use in the Olympic Yachting Games that will be a test of the competitors the equivalent of the test of that competition. It is also the consensus that the R.C.O. Secretariat-Wallah, being an ex-Rear-Commodore of the Yale Yacht Club, will ship a burgee of said Club for display alongside the collection to be seen in the next scene.

Scene 2:   Same hostelry – draught and dart room.
Time: High Tea.

As a result of a certain diurnal process, ascribable to the local statutes, the assemblage migrates across the hallway to engage in quaffing and a match of darts between Oxford and Poona teams each supplemented by memsahibs and sub-memsahibs. *The match threatens to last almost as long as the recent regatta so a second keg of bitters is tapped when suddenly it comes to a resounding conclusion in favour of the I.P.Y.C. when on the 12th round of play R.C.O. Secretariat-Wallah pierces the 'bull' with his second throw of the round – it should be noted that he had meticulously declined to play the red-feathered set, preferring those tipped in Yale blue.*

Scene 3:   No change in scene.
Time: Considerable change in time.
At this juncture all are feeling imperially to such a degree that it is the thinking, even among the backward races, that, since it is no longer possible to distinguish by their actions, graduate from undergraduate, or friend from foe, it is time to lower the curtain and thus conclude a most memorable occasion.

> *Too long constrain'd by civilization's traces,*
> *Let's seek surcease amongs't the Backwards Races.*

Perhaps unsurprisingly, this event has attracted some press coverage over the years, with varying degrees of amusement and understanding. The Tatler despatched a journalist and photographer for an article which appeared in the 15th November 1961 edition.

This was a sympathetic account which included the following:

Imperial Poona has an active list of about 25 headed by Prince Philip [to be explained in the next chapter]. *All of them are men who have made a name for themselves in competitive sailing and all of them have a passionate belief that sailing should be fun.... Boys of all ages who have fallen in love with boats assembled at the Perch, either to sail or to watch. There were the Poona people broad-shouldered with strong-boned faces and a couple of authoritatively greying hairs. The Oxford men were tall, wonderfully fit looking, and they all seemed to have those alert, restless eyes that don't easily let opportunity slip.... Dr Bennett was quickly in the lead. But a rowdy-looking Oxford boat came up and with remarkable fleetness and dexterity pinched the rudder! .....As the afternoon wore on the sheer indestructibility of English yachtsmen was manifestly apparent. Mr David Prior-Palmer, son of Sir Otho and a noted Christ Church skier and debater, was in a challenging position in an Oxford boat when he sat on a firework which propelled him into the river.*

The article even has photographic evidence of this last incident!

The Poona Team for the 1961 Backwards Races At Oxford

Back row: Brian Appleton, Mike Ford, Jamie Dobbs
Middle row: John Chamier, Noel Dobbs, Steven Longsdon, Peter Hunter, Hugh Somerville
Front row (prostrate): Reggie Bennett

A less sympathetic article appeared many years later in an Oxford newspaper when the author of this history was an undergraduate and organising the match. A friend, who wrote for this newspaper, wrote a fair account of the match, but his editor chose to modify it. The original piece was top and tailed with the following paragraphs:

Opening Paragraph
Oxford's reputation as a mecca for boorish aristocracy was confirmed on Sunday when members of the Imperial Poona Yacht Club caused heads to turn at The Perch public house in Binsey.

Closing Paragraph
Meanwhile, Oxford's jobless and homeless continue to increase.

It only remains for me to tail this account with the observation that the afore-mentioned editor was later required to spend time at the Her Majesty, the Queen Empress's, pleasure, which cannot, to my knowledge, be said of any member of the Imperial Poona Yacht Club!

The Backwards races took place in the 1950s and 60s, but the undergraduates lost interest for a period in the mid 1970s. They were revived in 1979 by Tony Lunch (who featured in Harry Anderson's play as an undergraduate) when Commodore of the OUYC. He was promptly elected a Poona member and appropriately called Tiffin. The races continued until the mid 1990s.

Silver Jubilee Dinner

This was held in The Royal Thames Yacht Club on 13th November 1959, with the original Commodore and joint-founder, Sir Archibald Hope, renewing his acquaintance with the Club and attending.

Imperial Poona Yacht Club Silver Jubilee Dinner, 13th November, 1959

Back row: Frank Murdoch, David Colville, Trevor de Hamel, Mike Ford, Sir Frank Spriggs, Brian Appleton, Glynn Blaxter, Jimmy Howden Hume, Charles Blake, Mike Parker
Middle row: Sir Heneage Ogilvie, Capt. Walter Rowe, Sir Archibald Hope, Prince Philip, Reggie Bennett, Rupert Kilkelly, Hugh Somerville, Osborne Dobell, Mike Crean, James Talbot, John Carew-Jones
Front row: Jim Orr, Joe Mellor, Uffa Fox, John Chamier

PRINCE PHILIP & HIS POT

A certain Prince Philip may have been noticed in the preceding photograph and his presence needs to be explained.

Reggie Bennett got to know Prince Philip through both being members of the Thursday Club. This was a club which consisted of around thirty scriptwriters, humorists and others, founded by a photographer called Baron, whose circle of friends, including Prince Philip, made up the Club. Reggie recalled that they met *"every Thursday with the ostensible reason of compelling the weekend to begin on Thursday lunchtime"* and that *"wit, of course, ran riot."*

The story goes that Reggie happened to be wearing a Poona tie (yellow, with red balls) one day, and Prince Philip asked him what club it was for. When Reggie replied that it was *"a load of balls"*, Prince Philip replied that he liked that and would like to join.

He was therefore elected an Honorary Member Extraordinary. (Reggie was quoted in the Daily Mail in August 1983 saying of the Imperial Poona Yacht Club: *"There are only 25 members and they all have to be fantastic sailors to qualify – Prince Philip is only an honorary member"*).

Being an honorary member did not, of course, prevent a Poona name being given, and he was grandly entitled His Highness The Maharaja of Cooch Parwani.

The Maharaja soon made a few suggestions for changes to the rules of the Club.

It may be recalled that these stated that membership would terminate automatically on *"ceasing to think Imperially"*. The Maharaja suggested that a footnote be added to the effect that *"ceasing to think shall not necessarily suspend or terminate membership"*.

The rules had also required every member present at a Tiffin to make a speech. John Chamier noted, in an article about the Club in the 1979 Christmas edition of The Field, a consequence of this: *"At one of these splendorous happenings one member of flag rank is noted as making the same speech three times before falling asleep at a fourth attempt."* (Reproduced with kind permission of The Field).

News of this, and possibly his experience of sitting through too many formal dinners, led the Maharaja to suggest the rule be changed to: *"At Tiffin every member present may be capable of speech."*

Both these rule changes were felt to be welcome additions to Poona's code and were adopted in 1955.

Two years later the Maharaja made perhaps his most significant contribution to the Club and, indeed, to sailing at Cowes, this being before the Cowes Combined Clubs Committee was formed. Reggie recalls that Prince Philip *"thought that the clubs at Cowes spent more time looking down their noses at one another rather than sailing against each other, so he presented a cup to make them sail against one another. So the five clubs at Cowes, of which Poona of course must be included, raced against each other for years and years."*

Uffa Fox, Tiny Mitchell, Reggie Bennett and David Colville met on 11th August 1957 to flesh out the idea, and Uffa sent the plan to Prince Philip, who was at Balmoral, the next day.

Five clubs were to be invited to participate:

> Royal Yacht Squadron
> Royal London Yacht Club
> Royal Corinthian Yacht Club
> Island Sailing Club
> Imperial Poona Yacht Club

The races were to be held in a selected one-design keelboat *"in the Solent during the Parliamentary recess, clear of Cowes Week."* Each club was to compete with a crew of amateur members of the club they represented.

These suggestions obviously met with royal approval, and the agreement of the clubs concerned, because the 1957 event was held in the International One Design Class under the burgee of the Royal Corinthian Yacht Club on Saturday 24th August and Sunday 25th August 1957.

The winning helmsman was to be awarded the HRH Prince Philip, Duke of Edinburgh's, Challenge Cup and the winning club the Imperial Poona Yacht Club Plaque.

Uffa Fox helmed the Imperial Poona Yacht Club team, with Reggie Bennett, John Chamier and Mike Ford as crew, to victory with three second places. A telegram was immediately despatched to Balmoral stating:

SAHIB'S SUPERIOR SAILING SKILL SECURES PRINCE PHILIP'S POONA POT

The next day Uffa wrote a long account of the event for Prince Philip. His covering letter read:

My Dear Prince Philip,

This is a very long letter giving a true and faithful report of the first series of races that you have invented for us. I would like you not to attempt to read it until you have half an hour or so to while away and then you can picture us storming round the courses, sometimes in charge of the I.O.D.'s and sometimes the I.O.D.'s taking charge of us.

I hope you will enjoy all this and if you only get one hundredth part of fun out of imagining our struggles as we slashed through the seas, it will be well worth my while writing this description.

Best wishes,

Yours ever

Uffa

With such a billing from Uffa, it is only right to include his full account here.

Saturday 24th August came in with a westerly gale that continued throughout the day, which meant that each of the three races would be full of zest, zip and demand a great deal of skill and seamanship on the part of the helmsmen and crews in order to sail the boats round the course under full sail, and the other four boats in the race would increase the intensity of the struggle.

The first course set was K. All marks to port, Prince Consort, East Bramble, West Bramble, East Gurnard to line.

The boats, the International One Design, a Six Metre type hull with a cabin top, with a lead keel, a large mainsail and a small jib and no runners to work. Fast, sensible and seaworthy boats that could be driven to the utmost and still survive.

There were to be five races in five boats and the complete crew, with helmsmen, to change boats at every race.

I am the helmsman of the Imperial Poona Yacht Club boat with Doctor Reginald Bennett, John Chamier and Michael Ford as crew. The first boat we are in is Two Ton Tiny Mitchell's Boat, "Windflower", No. 10.

The start is a run and so we decide to be the outer boat and reach out across the line, keeping just the right side of it until the gun goes, when we shall square right away and set the spinnaker. We have an ebb tide taking us to the westward and so keeping us the right side of the line, so can be hard up on the line all the way out. One of my crew, at one moment, suggested that I could get a bit closer to the line but I pointed out to him that we were laying down at fifty and sixty degrees, according to the squalls, and he in the centre line of the boat had to take into allowance the fact that our great long mast was a long way to leeward of his eyes, that any part of the boat over the line would cause us to be recalled.

We made the best start and our spinnaker was going up with smoke still showing from the gun. Then Bobbie Lowein, the steersman of the Island Sailing Club's boat, "Margaret", No. 7, started to luff across our stern and if we had to respond to his luff, we should have soon been in great trouble with our spinnaker and so I let him go to windward. The effect of this was that he shielded some of the wind out of our spinnaker while it was being set and so helped, instead of hindering, as was his plan, the setting of our spinnaker.

Away we went at a terrific pace for the East Bramble Buoy, four mile dead to leeward.

The different boats in the fleet set their spinnakers and soon the lot of us were rolling and tearing along through the water, making a vigorous and exciting picture.

About a third of the way to the buoy our spinnaker halyard parted with a bang, but we had this aboard before it could get under water and my crew had actually started to take in the spinnaker, but I said, "Oh no. Up you go Michael and re-reeve the spinnaker halyard." So up Michael went, while Reggie Bennett muzzled the spinnaker on deck. To make Michael's work of climbing the mast a little easier, I luffed as soon as they had drawn up level with us across the stern of the Royal Yacht Squadron's boat, for this did two things. It cut their wind, got them interested in a little luffing match and also laid the boat down to an angle so that the mast was about thirty degrees from the upright, instead of being plumb, so making it easier to climb, and also meant that we were going into less tide, which was against us, and if there was any advantage, we should have the inside turn at the mark when we came upon it.

It was quite a struggle for Michael up the mast, but he finally rove off the spinnaker halyard, but just as he came down below the cross-tree I saw that it was round the jumper stays, so he had to climb back another six feet to reeve it off clear. That was the hardest bit of his climb. Down he came, and making fast the spinnaker halyard, soon had the spinnaker set again and away we ran for the buoy. As we came near the buoy, we were running quite dead, I gybed over on to the starboard tack once the spinnaker had come down and so had the right of way as well as calling for room at the mark, and we rounded the mark in third place, with two boats well ahead of us.

It was quite an exciting mark as we had to gybe and then come right up close hauled and tack immediately we could – all of which was carried out successfully and soon we were standing over to the Island shore and a stronger fair tide on the starboard tack. The two boats ahead soon followed.

As we stood on and on across, I eased the jib just a little and the main a bit more, for there was far more than these boats could stand in the steep Solent seas, with this weight of wind. We forged our way through the fleet and went to windward.

Meanwhile, John Chamier, who was on the mainsheet, and myself, looked and looked and looked for the West Bramble Buoy – our next mark, but never did once see it. The result was we overstood by something like quarter of a mile and this dropped us back into second place where we stayed for the hard reach across from the West Bramble, with the west going tide, to the East Gurnard, and then a run from the East Gurnard up over the line with the spinnaker set fairly close in shore to avoid the worst of the tide.

One or two of the boats had sustained damage in their spinnaker gear, and only enthusiasts would have set spinnakers on such a day, and so we decided not to have two races in the morning but two in the afternoon and to get these things put right while we were enjoying our lunch.

Meantime, one of the boats had to be replaced by Jack Harrison's brand-new I.O.D., and as all the rigging was unstretched and the sails quite new, Jack thought that he would like to steer his boat so that, if anyone carried the mast away, it would be him.

So for the second race, the Great Gorgeous Rear, John Chamier, stood down for the Gross Vater Colonel Jack Harrison and I came off the tiller and went on to the mainsheet.

Because of the gale, the Starting Committee wisely decided to send us on a very short and easy course for the middle race so that we could endure and the boats endure for the final race, which would be a hard one.

This second course set, was the reverse of E. Line, to Old Castle Point, Thorn Knoll, East Gurnard and the Line. Again, the start was off the wind but this time it was a broad reach with no spinnakers to be set. We all arrived at Old Castle Point in a heap with the Island Sailing Club's boat just ahead and we the second boat round, and being a reach, we continued in this order round the course until the finish, for it was a close reach across to Thorn Knoll, a reach back to the East Gurnard, and a short run home to the finish.

We had our spinnaker on the bow already to set and the halyard attached by one of the Swedish snap-hooks that when you press a button spring open, but these often have a dreadful knack of springing themselves open. This one did this and as Reggie Bennett hoisted away on the halyard, all he did was to take the halyard aloft and not the sail. So we had to finish and keep our second place without a spinnaker and we managed to do this by getting close up under the rocks and in out of the tide, so that no-one else could get to weather of us, and being less tide, also take our wind. Once again, the Imperial Poona boat was second, and, once again, the Island Sailing Club's boat was first.

Now came the final race of the day. By now, it was blowing harder than ever. Reggie Bennett went to the Island Sailing Club's crew and said would they mind Jack Harrison steering his own boat as it was all new and he was afraid of the rigging going, or something carrying away, but they, being very earnest about the race, said "No", and that as Jack had seen the mast stand for one race he thought it was all right for the next and so Bobbie Lowein steered the Island Sailing Club's boat in the third race of the day.

We could almost lay the first mark from the weather end of the line but in here there was little fair tide although we were right up in the weather berth, but for all that I decided to start in there, but through interference with other boats, we started with little or no way on but, even so, in this weight of wind, there was enough wind in-shore to keep us in the weather berth and in the first place.

Meantime, out to leeward in a strong fair tide, Paddy Quennell was driving along at a great speed in Tiny Mitchell's boat and when he tacked he would be on starboard tack with right of way, which is worth always three boats length and on such an exciting day as this, perhaps even more.

Immediately he tacked, although he was a long way away, I also tacked to starboard so that I could tack for the buoy well clear of anyone else, and planned to give myself enough room to go under Paddy Quennell's stern on the starboard tack, slide through his lee and so make the buoy first, he having to give me room at the mark even if I had not got through his lee. There are very few people in this world who can resist crossing another boat on the starboard tack when they have right of way, but here Paddy showed great restraint and judgement for, as we approached him on the port tack, he went about before we arrived, knowing that he could make the mark, and I, diving away to go under his stern, when my crew yelled that he had got into irons, so we luffed up our stem, missing his stern by the thickness of a cigarette paper, and away we went to windward of him and on around the mark ahead.

At the mark, the main sheet could not be eased and I was unable to hold our boat "Arrow", No. 5, out of the wind, and so we reached across for Calshot instead of being able to make our gybe round the buoy and run up for the Prince Consort on the starboard gybe, in out of the worst of the tide.

Meanwhile, Paddy Quinnell had rounded the buoy and, being in a little less tide than us, soon came up abreast and made gybing impossible until he did. Now, instead of sailing at the Prince Consort buoy, we are sailing a course forty-five degrees from it, at the Calshot Lightship.

I pointed out to Paddy that we were miles off course and that we *could not gybe until he did, and eventually he gybed and in doing so tore some bits out of "Windflower's" sail and then we gybed without damage, so all was well as far as the first two boats were concerned.*

Meantime, the Royal London Yacht Club boat, instead of gybing, had gone about to come through the wind to get on to the other gybe and so dropped further astern.

Bobbie Lowein, sailing Jack Harrison's new boat, failed to get the mainsail off the crosstrees and so, when he gybed, split the mainsail and had to give up. We, of course, were delighted that he was out of the race and thought this was nothing but justice and it meant that we would be in the lead for points.

Meanwhile, Paddy Quennell's boat "The Pirate", sailed by the Royal Yacht Squadron's team, was chasing away before the wind and heading straight for the Brambles. She did a gybe, but only half of the sail went over as the top half was caught on the crosstree, so they gybed back again to clear this and, after sometime, finally decided to put her through the wind instead of gybing and eventually came round and on to the course for the Peel Bank buoy. Here was Paddy, the owner of the boat, close aboard us trying to sail Tiny Mitchell's "Windflower" into first place and, at the same time, wondering, first of all, if his own boat, "Pirate II" would survive the two Chinese gybes and being quite certain in his own mind that, if she did, she would finally finish up a wreck on the Brambles itself. However, all was well, and she finished the course safely without any damage.

Meantime, we were roaring away through Cowes Road, diving our bows under seas, so much so, that our Pilgrim Father, the masthead man wanted to go forward to get the spinnaker off the stemhead, but I pointed out to him that once we had passed Old Castle Point, the wind would be across the tide, we should have smoother water and might set the spinnaker. At this time we were the leading boat, but some-how or another Paddy Quennell sailed Tiny's boat ahead of us, although to leeward. This meant, that, for some strange reason, Tiny's boat went faster than the rest and that as soon as we had the opportunity, we had to put up the spinnaker to get on equal terms with her. So we started a little luffing to get them interested in this and to get into a position where our spinnaker would pay us better and while they were interested in luffing our masthead man nipped forward, put the spinnaker boom on the spinnaker and up she went. Just as it was up and set, a hell of a squall hit us and I had to use all my strength to keep the boat from broaching, for if she had brought this squall abeam with a spinnaker up she would certainly have filled and sank as there was nothing I could see we could do to save her from being blown over on to her beam ends. So away we chased to leeward of Paddy and quite soon we were abreast of him. Then the squall eased, but only for about thirty seconds, then down came another even harder one. We tore along with spray flying everywhere and everything strained to the utmost. So I decided that directly this squall had ended we would get the spinnaker down as it had done the job it was put up for, and that was to get us ahead of Paddy and I knew we would only have something like thirty seconds or so in which to get the spinnaker down between this and the next squall. With a good crew, however, this was no worry, and directly the squall eased, Michael nipped forward, unclipped the spinnaker off the fore end of the boom, while John gathered in to leeward and Reggie Bennett lowered it away, so we had it in the cabin in the twinkling of an eye and Michael could take his spinnaker boom off calmly and quietly – at least so it seemed after the wild rush we had with the spinnaker set. Even so, we had all the wind the boat wanted.

Now we started to luff up through to come out ahead of "Windflower" and to lead him round the Peel Bank buoy, but "Windflower's" superior speed stopped us doing this, so seeing that we would go round the buoy outside and under his lee, I bore right away so that I should be approaching the buoy on a close reach and would only have to luff up a little bit to get her right on to the wind and headed into Osborne Bay, while Paddy, approaching the buoy and having to turn at a very acute angle, would have no time to gather his sheets, and we could either go through his lee or to weather of him, whichever was best. Sure enough, they could not round too quickly and they left a gap of about twenty-five feet between them and the buoy with no chance at all of luffing in that weight of wind as even if they pointed the boat up, she would not go there, because of the windage in the mast and hull. So we darted through, just missing the buoy, well to windward, and the pair of us stood inshore to Osborne Bay, we gradually eating out to windward on the way in.

When in, both stood around on the port tack and up for the Old Castle Point, with Paddy some fifty yards astern. So we sailed, having to ease both the jib and the mainsheet in the heaviest of squalls to prevent the boat laying down on her beam ends and filling, for the squalls came down over the high lands of Osborne House, and flattened us out when they hit us.

Meantime, Dick Freemantle, steering "Margaret", No. 7, had stood round earlier under our lee and able to lay Castle Point, gained quite a bit on us, and so we arrived at Old Castle Point with the Poona in the lead, the Royal Corinthian next and the Royal London next, all of us, with only a half boat's length of water between us.

We all made a short one into the shore and then came about for the line and as we went along, Paddy Quennell in Tiny's boat decided to bear off to leeward, reach harder and go through our lee and I would dearly have loved to have borne away on top of him. The laws of sailing say that, while you can luff a man head to wind if he tries to pass you to windward, you should give him a free passage to leeward. So we held our course while Paddy slowly and surely sailed through our lee, and because the Starting Line and the Finishing Line points to the east a little, it meant that even if he was only abeam of us, he would get the gun first. So we came to the Finish with all the advantages in favour of Paddy, who had now pulled out with a clear wind to leeward.

I was sure that he was the winner, but we always live in hope, and arrived at shore to find that Paddy had won by one second, about a quarter of a boat's length, then the Royal London about four boat lengths astern and the Royal Yacht Squadron possibly a quarter of a mile astern of that.

So ended the day's racing with the Imperial Poona Yacht Club ahead on points.

We had a most enjoyable dinner after a bath at the Corinthian Yacht Club, and so to bed.

The following morn, I was awakened by a telephone call to say that a gale, force eight, was predicted for the day, and the postponement signal was hoisted, but by ten o'clock the owners of the boats had decided that the weather was not fit and so the Imperial Poona team settled down to some quiet drinks at eleven a.m., in my home. It was quite simple. Young Michael Ford, the measthead man, went for Madeira so all I had to do was to give him a glass and a bottle. Reggie decided on gin and sweet martini, and so he had two bottles, and John Chamier decided on the same thing, so he had two bottles, and I had my bottle of sherry, so we could all pour out our drinks as required and yarn about all sorts of things from my choir boy days to sailing on the day before.

Just before the sun was over the yard arm, we went along to the Corinthian Club to fill Prince Philip's Poona Pot – marvellous great tankard, beautiful to look at, to drink from, dating from George II, held two bottles of champagne comfortably. We filled the thing three times and then Tiny filled it with a wonderful mixture of vintage port and a wonderful old brandy. Both of them so mellow that they slid down like mother's milk and they were so potent that at dinner that night afterwards, Tiny complained that he had had no lunch, although he had had, to my knowledge, some wonderful beef, after melon, and finished with a great chunk of stilton cheese.

So ended the first races between the Clubs of Cowes.

After some recommendations for the following year, Uffa concludes:

These are my thoughts and also the story of the first series of races in the contest you have so brilliantly invented for us. I have never had so much fun sailing in any one day before and Bobby Lowein, who steered the Island Sailing Club's boat, came in for a drink this lunchtime on the Monday and he also said the same thing, and so we think that this new set of races will develop into the most important series of races in the country and possibly the world, and at the same time, be the greatest fun for all.

Thank you very much indeed for all the joy it has brought into the hearts of the twenty people who took part in it and also for the joy it has brought to Tiny Mitchell who is largely responsible for carrying out your ideas.

The event was clearly considered a success and repeated. The last placed club was responsible for organising the following year's races, so it was fortunate that Poona never lost, because the lack of a clubhouse or boats in the continent of Europe may have hindered proceedings somewhat.

The Island Sailing Club won in 1958 and 1959, but Poona was back victorious in 1960. The following year, the Royal London Yacht Club changed the event from fleet to match racing, with Prince Philip's approval, and the Royal Yacht Squadron won under this new format.

However, the Squadron's time at the top of the pile was short lived when they were last in 1962 and Poona victorious for the third time. Once again telegrams were exchanged:

To Buckingham Palace: *POONA WON POT BY ONE POINT.*

From Buckingham Palace: *FELICITATIONS. IF PRESSED WILL SEND SMALL TIN OF CURRY POWDER FOR CELEBRATION TIFFIN. COOCH PARWANI.*

However, this exchange of telegrams caused quite an episode as Reggie described in a letter to the palace:

I sent the telegram to Prince Philip before I left [on holiday], *little thinking that it would arouse such a hullabaloo indirectly as that which faced me on my return.*

I rang up the Postmaster to say he could start delivering letters again and he said that both he and the police had been trying to deliver a telegram they could not understand from someone they could not quite place but emanating from Buckingham Palace Post Office.

Poona was back in winning form in 1965 and won the event the following two years as well. With three victories in a row, Poona claimed that they had won the Cup outright and handed it back to the Maharaja who promptly represented it.

The original five clubs continued to compete in the event, with the losing club acting as host, until 1973 when it moved to Bembridge, was sailed in the club boats and expanded to involve all the sailing clubs based on the Isle of Wight and, of course, Poona.

The Poona Team at the Prince Philip Pot, 1970

Crew: Mike Ford, Nevill Ambler, Malcolm Green

RAIDS ON DEAUVILLE

In the 1960s, the Club was privileged to hoist the three balls up the mast of the Maharaja's yacht 'Bloodhound' and sail across the channel to the republic of France.

Before the first of these outings, a telegram was received by the yacht's Sailing Master at 6.30pm on 7th May 1964:

THE MAHARAJA OF COOCH PARWANI SENDS THE MEMBERS OF THE LOWER ORDERS OF THE IMPERIAL POONA YACHT CLUB AT PRESENT MORE OR LESS IN CHARGE OF BLOODHOUND A MESSAGE OF FEARFUL GREETINGS STOP HE CANNOT UNDERSTAND HOW BLOODHOUND GOT INTO THEIR HANDS AND HE PRAYS TO THE GOD SINKNOT THAT WHATEVER HAPPENS TO THE MEMBERS BLOODHOUND WILL RETURN SAFELY AFTER THIS HAZARDOUS EXPEDITION

Poona responded to such wishes in imperial style, as is detailed in the report written by Reggie:

BLOODHOUND TO DEAUVILLE
I.P.Y.C.
8 – 11 MAY 1964

There joined: *Commodore Bennett Sahib (Reggie Bennett)*
Baby Blake (Charles Blake)
Pilgrim Father (Mike Ford)
Yeti (Brian Appleton)
Sowar ke Batcha (Noel Dobbs)
Donkeyman (Malcolm Green)

As it was more or less blowing the roof off and the forecasters were predicting force 8 in all areas as a start, blowing up to forces 9-10 up north, discretion prevailed on Friday afternoon, 8th, and the sahibs contented themselves with erecting their yak-skin tents all over the ship. Brian Yeti had been given leave to arrive late, and by the time he arrived, about 7.30, the wind and the forecasters, and indeed the sahibs, were all considerably less windy and 'Bloodhound' proceeded immediately, logging 9.3 miles in the first hour from moorings in a rousing SW breeze that gave a close fetch on a course of 160° magnetic from Fort Blockhouse to Deauville west pierhead.

By midnight we were through the mid-Channel steamship lane, still logging over 9 knots. The efficacy of Bloodhound's navigation lights was simply demonstrated by the way the shipping scattered at our approach, even on a moonless night. We were going as fast as they were, anyway, which must have puzzled them.

In the small hours, as we entered the bay of the Seine, the wind dropped right away to a flat calm. Under all plain power 'Bloodhound' steamed into a cloudless sunny morning, picking up Havre L.V. at 0600 and squeaking through Deauville lock gates with only eight minutes to spare before closing time (of the lock, of course).

Squeaking is perhaps the wrong word so far as the sound is concerned, for Henri Millet, the Commodore of Deauville Y.C., and Pierre Faure Beaulieu, the Secretary, were lurking on the gate-side, wreathed in diabolical leers whose cause was soon to be revealed. A 'appy little belch, like, and there sailed up a couple of hundred feet a small black object which exploded with a stunning crash – a lifeboat maroon!

A series of these tremendous air-bursts helped us up-harbour, leaving Deauville quaking with fright. We moored up neatly with our stern to the Club itself, that elegantly converted 'blockaus' of the Organization Todt.

Now started the social whirl, 23 ½ hours of it. It may not have been original, but it was very nice to enjoy. An immediate visit to the club was soon superseded by an invitation to the Vice-President's villa at the other end of Deauville. Francis and John took watches, alternating as socialite and cookie. Francis was the socialite at lunch time.

As the hospitality asserted itself, the leers of the younger members became less inhibited and so did their French language. All hands were capable of quite a good stream before the day was over.

After luncheon on board, hands enjoyed a fairly lengthy zizzex on deck in the sun but the afternoon was enlivened by a visit from a solemn young Customs officer who came to inspect the ship's passport, a new idea. There were a few questions to be answered and the sahibs gathered to help him. Ship's name? Difficult to spell in French but could be done. Owner? We looked at one another and told him. "La Reine d'Angleterre?" "That's right." Next question – Age? Ship's Age of Construction? No, age of the proprietaire. Such an un-Sahib-like question got no very clear answer, and suddenly the officer picked up his papers and started off ashore, asserting, "Ce n'est pas un rigolade   " etc. etc. etc. as it all faded into the distance. We had pressed Lloyds Register, duly engraved, upon him to no avail. He made two later rather incoherent and excited visits before somebody in his office must have told him – as nobody on the club quay seemed prepared to do. They weren't going to spoil the fun!

The evening held a Yacht Club reception at 6.30 and a reception at the Casino at 10. But we anticipated and asked the Club officers and other old friends aboard at 5.45, as they were dying to come. The Sous-Prefet from Lisieux, and the Mayor and Contesse d'Ornano came too – she remembered our Pilgrim Father when 'Mayflower' arrived in America, so Mike Ford was a bit above himself for the rest of the evening. This very attractive mayoress and her husband spoke English with ease, as did about half the members, so, apart from a speech of welcome from Max Boiteau, the Club President, and a reply in the Commodore Sahib's best fractured French and Hindustani, communications were easy.

Dinner on board (Francis' turn) was enlivened by a few light-hearted somersaults by the Baby Blake who had earlier delighted the French by appearing in his formal topee and other regalia. Then to the final "champagne d'honneur" at the Casino, given by Jacques Gilbert, the Directeur. Here, in the absence of some of the distractions during the earlier proceedings, the Sahibs turned their attention to the tables and the other distractions surrounding these.

On Sunday morning, after some final purchases of postcards, croissants and other consumable stores, the Sahibs bade farewell to the D.Y.C.'s braves and proceeded to sea at 9.30, with one final and highly un-sabbatarian conclusion. A weak cold front had cleared the sky and left a light breeze in NW, of all places! So we slowly stood out past Le Havre on port tack and settled down to a whole day's flat calm and basking some 10 miles north of Havre. An engine run across Channel brought us into the next gathering warm front, and Bloodhound stormed in from the Owers at a good 10 knots with mizzen staysail set, mooring up just before 5 a.m. on Monday.

The operation, ambitious as it was, went without a hitch and must have given greater pleasure to more participants than any but a few of its kind. The atmosphere on board was quite delightful. The gratitude of the Sahibs knows no bounds and is most emphatically and even violently expressed. It was a huge privilege and a great joy. We would like to give something to the ship to express our feelings – but she is so beautifully found that it is difficult to think of anything not actually useless. We shall hope to be able to entertain the gallant Sailing Master to tiffin in due course, and meanwhile we should like to express to our Maharaja and to his Maharanee our delightful thanks for the treat they have given us.

It may seem odd, but among the remarkably Imperial thinkers of Deauville it does seem that a Republican Cell may well have been started by the visit of a Royal Yacht.

Another raid on Deauville was made in 1967, although Reggie Bennett was not present. The third trip was the last voyage made by 'Bloodhound' before she was disposed of by her owners. It also marked the foundation of another Outpost of the Club.

It is clearly important that the report of a trip with such dual historical importance is recorded in full:

I.P.Y.C BLOODHOUND TO DEAUVILLE
$10^{th}/13^{th}$ *October, 1969.*

The last cruise of Bloodhound was by a felicitous coincidence allotted to the Imperial Poona Yacht Club, at least Poona thinks it was felicitous. No less than nine Sahibs were accommodated, "hot bunk" principle; This was found acceptable in the absence of the Haro-bhoi (Rule 18).

The Sahibs were led by the Commode, Baby Blake and Mike Ford (Pilgrim Father) as watchkeepers, together with Brian Appleton (Yeti or Abominable Snowman), Noel Dobbs (Sowar Ke Batcha), Peter Hunter (Babun), Malcolm Green (Donkeyman), Johnsons Wooderson (Ramm of Kutch) and Nevill Ambler (Chapatty).

This allowed three watches of three, in three-hour watches, and proved a most agreeable arrangement while David Gay, Mike and Paul were able to be idlers (although not especially idle!).

I joined the ship about 12.30 on Friday and Baby Blake and I were hardly even outside our first gin when a blanket of fog, such as had been investing the Home Counties since dawn, suddenly rolled up and enveloped us. No half measures. It was there to stay. All hands joined, however, in some miraculous way and at 3.00 p.m. we slipped and proceeded.

We had seen the last of terra firma. We saw neither side as we left harbour and we only dimly saw the Isle of Wight boat as it crept in through the Spring ebb. We whirled merrily down the Channel skipping from buoy to buoy while the fog dripped heavily down the back-stays and soaked everybody. We even had to rig a dodger on the pulpit to try and keep our forward lookout dry as he stood up there with the sparklet hooter. The last buoy we saw was Warner and soon even the sun was obscured as the fog bank thickened. This remained so until the approach of evening when the sun gradually began to be seen at a much lower angle of sight and finally our radius of vision began to increase as darkness began to fall. We motored merrily on with the Poona flag blowing out bravely in the floodlight at the masthead. A light easterly air got up as the fog thinned and we were able to keep the mainsail and jib full, this adding a knot to our speed.

The night watches were fortunately pretty clear and in the Middle not one ship was sighted. Towards morning the engine was stopped for a while and the ship was making over five knots with the sails just nicely free. As dawn came up at about 6.00 a.m., Le Havre lightship was sighted, only to vanish suddenly when about a 100 degrees off as thick fog came down again. This continued throughout our approach to the land but we picked up the Fairway buoy for Deauville and felt our way inshore, while the bleat of the foghorn boomed round the horizon to mislead us. By and by we saw that the sea appeared to be streaming in the chilly atmosphere and leads began to show through the banks along to port, a rift in the bank suddenly disclosed the roof of the Normandy Hotel which was instantly recognised by the more experienced hands. The kedge was dropped forthwith and breakfast was served at 8.30.

We entered harbour at 09.30 in clear air and a light southerly breeze, announcing our arrival with a feu-de-joy from our large mortar on the foredeck with coloured star shell. We were berthed alongside the club house where we divided our attention between hygiene and Ricard.

The Deauville Yacht Club had been specially reopened for us and Madame Lucien had even returned from the South of France to dispense to us. Commodore Henry Millet, the Mayor of the nearby metropolis of Blonville, duly received us together with a number of his hospitable colleagues shortly to be enrolled in this Section Batard Normand. M. Miguet, the Sous Prefet from Lisieux, another prospective member of the Section visited the ship with his wife, and Johnson Wooderson's shifting into shore-going clothes was much admired. Nevill Ambler met again two ladies who had been introduced to him on a previous visit as marriageable playmates, until he visited their homes and met their husbands and numerous families. These ladies, Madame Pruvost and Madame Martinache, were indeed the life and soul of the party at all times. It need only be said that their husbands were present so that such people as Hunter were restrained to some extent.

In the evening Commodore Millet and the Club entertained Bloodhound to a delightful little Champagne party at which of course many of the Poonas as well as the Bloodhound were meeting old friends from earlier visits or from earlier contests.

The party adjourned to the nearby Ocean Hotel, where Charlie Blake had set himself up in splendour, and nineteen people sat down to a very fine cous-cous which just about knocked everybody out. It is regrettable to have to report that Brian Appleton was laid low with a stomach upset apparently deriving from his original upset at Zermatt some years ago, but it is equally regrettable that Charlie Blake's topee proved not to be waterproof, to the detriment of Suzanne Millet who was sitting alongside him; that Malcolm Green played a highly successful custard-pie act at Peter Hunter's expense, and that Peter Hunter chose to entertain the assembled company from the middle of the table with a song and story, in what can only be described as his appalling taste. It was all the more unfortunate that in the restaurant there was a gentleman from Paris who had come to Deauville for a quiet weekend away from his wife and family and was dining alone and communing with his own spirit. He did not have much of a chance against the enthusiastic expressions of sympathy showered upon him, which were no more helpful than Hunter's somewhat off colour performance. The evening ended at a discotheque nearby in the heat and almost total darkness lit from time to time by the fluorescent brilliance of the chef's tall hat worn by Commodore Millet in the light of the ultra-violet transmitters. A toast was proposed by Henry Millet to the Queen-Empress, to which I responded with a toast to the President of France and "L' empereur en retraite".

  Next morning Charlie Blake entertained all hands to breakfast at the Ocean Hotel, which had also been opened especially for the occasion of our visit. After a short visit to the town for a little shopping, the Sahibs assembled on board at 11.00 to receive their French friends.

  It was a cool and brightly sunny morning with the same light easterly air, and Bloodhound's deck was soon fully occupied by a party. Among the further Deauvillains were the monstrous Pierre Lepeudry, that particularly dangerous helmsman Pierre Frottie and young Jean-Pierre Millet, who on hearing of our arrival had come up from Paris specially this morning. It was a splendid concourse of people, very largely old friends and almost entirely the prospective members of the Section Batard Normand, which was hereby inaugurated. The title is of course the reference to a Duke, whose parentage has always been impuned by history, who lived a mile or two from Deauville and gate crashed his way into England in 1066. No reflection is intended on any other Dukes or indeed on any other Normans!

  The foundation membership of the Section comprises:

    Sous-Prefet R. Miguet
    Commodore Henry Millet
    Pierre Frottie
    Pierre Lepeudry
    M. Martinache
    M. Pruvost
    Jean-Pierre Millet

all of whom were present, together with the Depute et Maire of Deauville, Michel d'Ornano, the President of the D.Y.C., Maitre Max Boiteau, and the secretary of the D.Y.C. Pierre Faure-Beaulieu, which last three were unable to be present.

It was decided to try and hold a tiffin in London in late November if possible and one at the Sous-Prefecture at Lisieux next Easter.

Now the party began to break up. Commodore Millet and one or two others had guests coming to lunch, but the remainder, particularly the girls, were retained on board while the ship let go of the quay and proceeded out of the basin before the tide should neap her on the way out. The signal for departure was a series of thunderous explosions from the mortars and maroons at the Club House, together with the end-of-commission expenditure of pyrotechnic stores, being particularly admired, and the red smoke generators making it almost impossible for David Gay to find the hole in the granite from which to head for the open sea, the following wind keeping the smoke clouds accurately over the ship. No incidents are to be reported with the customs or any other services on this visit, and so no repercussions need to be expected from this direction on this occasion.

Bloodhound kedged to seaward of the pierhead and the party continued. As the champagne began to run low, however, parties of our guests began to be put ashore together with the last of the glasses borrowed from the Club.

A somewhat carefree lunch was taken on deck in the sunshine, Charlie Blake still in his full rig and Hunter as usual disgracing himself with the brandy.

At 14.45 the mainsail was hoisted and the kedge recovered and the great downhill rush across the Channel began, with the Genoa boomed out to starboard and a very healthy breeze going, so speeds were from seven to nine knots and more throughout the afternoon, evening and night. The Owers was sighted at 01.00, Bembridge Ledge was abeam at 04.00 and at 05.55 Bloodhound ran herself firmly on the putty less than a length from her berth in the Cold-harbour. The Sahibs dispersed and Bloodhound herself prepared for her slipping and survey at the end of the most glorious end to a most fabulous career.

It must be claimed that the end surpassed any possible glories at any other time, and to say that the Sahibs are grateful is a woeful understatement. They hurl themselves prostrate, heaving loads of dust and ashes over themselves in their expressions of gratitude to the owners, for being so generous and indeed so trusting as to allow so precious a ship into the hands of such an unprincipled gang of villains.

BACK IN BLIGHTY

The previous two chapters have shown the Imperial Poona Yacht Club in rude health in the 1960s, often ruling the waves in Cowes and possibly waiving the rules in Deauville (certainly according to the hard pressed custom's official!). This state of activity continued into the 1970s, although the Club had to do its irreverent bit to keep up with the times.

Rule Changes

The introduction of the Race Relations Acts 1964-70 resulted in an additional clause in the Club's rules: *"For 'white' read 'black' and for 'coloured' read 'coloured' throughout."*

Voting for the Flag Officers was so tight in 1970 that, instead of just a Great White Vice, an additional post of Great Black Vice was also created, again acknowledging the recent legislation.

Further legislation in 1978 (and anticipating more) required another change (as is stated in the Club's rules) *"in order to conform to the relevant legislation, to wit the Abolition of Sex Differentiation Act 1978, the Parthenogenesis Act 1979, the Androgyny Act 1980 and the Universal Hermaphroditism Act 1984: Rule 6, last sentence, shall be deemed to read 'No memsahib, male or female, is eligible'."*

Fractured Spar

A regular contest against the Flying Fifteen fleet at the newly-founded Grafham Water Sailing Club was introduced in April 1967, and the Fractured Spar trophy was sailed for on many occasions in the late 1960s and early 1970s. This explains the Poona flag in the bar of that land-locked club.

40th Anniversary Tiffin

For the Club's 40th anniversary, in 1974, members were privileged to be invited for a Tiffin onboard the Maharaja's Imperial Dhow, Britannia, on Sunday 4th August 1974 during Cowes Week.

While Poona could be accused of many things, being ostentatious is perhaps not one of them – it is quite possibly the only club where an invitation to such a special dinner could be sent out by the club's secretary in a hand written and photocopied note!

But the sahibs responded and had a magnificent evening.

By this time, Uffa Fox, who had been the Maharaja's sailing companion during Cowes Week for many years, had died and Reggie

Bennett had taken his place in this role, regularly staying on board for the week.

Abdul Gunneybags

Perhaps as a result of word of this honoured occasion reaching the back streets of the sub-continent, in March 1975, Reggie received certain documents from an immigrant from Bombay which appeared to be a request for membership from someone called Abdul Gunneybags, who claimed to be a Bandari Wallah (with much acclaim for his curry and samoosas) as well as having sea experience.

Enclosed with this begging letter were what can only be described as a sheaf of spurious references to his skills as a cook / bearer from previous employers in Bombay.

However, despite all this, when his possible candidature was circulated to the members, no black topees were received. Indeed, the Great Gorgeous Rear, John Chamier, replied with some support to his application, writing *"he has a yacht aboard which he got lost and since it only sails against the sun he was forced to go on till he got back."* He was, of course, the first person to do this single-handed and non-stop.

His election was approved, but not without serious reservations from the Maharaja, who described him as a *"miserable sea cook"*! Nevertheless, Abdul, with tales of his time in India, and bottle of lime pickle, is always an entertaining participant at any Tiffin, often in partnership with the Serang, Nevill Ambler, who can also recount tales of the sub-continent.

Poona And The SINS

Abdul's election was just in time, because that summer there was the London Festival of Sail and he, under his slightly more conventional name of Robin Knox-Johnston, happened to be manager of the St. Katherine's Yacht Haven.

He organised a match, on Wednesday 27th August 1975, between the forty year old Imperial Poona Yacht Club and a recently formed group who called themselves the SINS. This stood for the Society of International Nautical Scribes. This event was described in the Peterborough column of The Daily Telegraph as *"without question the oddest event during the Port of London Clipper Regatta."*

As one would expect from the groups concerned, and Abdul's involvement, the rules for this event contained some entertaining elements:

The starting signals: *A topee will be held aloft at the five minute signal, and will be lowered for the start roughly in time with the start signal. If these two signals do not coincide, discretion may be used as to which start signal is used, subject to the Race Officer not changing his mind afterwards.*

The scoring system: *The IPYC shall be deemed to be the winners unless the protest committee decide otherwise upon receipt of a properly phrased protest which should include suitably compelling evidence and a protest fee of 8 Annas.*

Penalty points: *In the event of arrest of any of the competitors, each team shall be responsible for bail of its own members.*

The report of the event in Yachts & Yachting (which is reprinted with their kind permission) read:

Two Lasers per side were used, the race was a relay and the course was a figure of eight around the bascules of Tower Bridge. It has to be recorded that the Harbour Master and River Police were very tolerant of the whole affair, incredulous as they were of the persistence of a constant stream of different helmsmen in widely varying attire making repeated passes at the traffic in the London River's main fairway.

The SINS team, having scored a resounding conquest, were declared the victors – despite a clause in the racing instructions which stated clearly that the Poona should be declared the winners. The latter, it was suspected, had wind of the fact that the first prize was a bottle of White Horse whisky, albeit a very large one, while second prize was a crate of bubbly.

Jubilee River Pageant and Fireworks

The following year the Queen Empress celebrated her Golden Jubilee and it was felt appropriate that Poona marked this occasion. There was nowhere better to do this than at the heart of government.

Poona was not alone in this gathering, organised by Reggie – they were joined by members of the Royal Thames Yacht Club and the House of Commons Yacht Club. However, their presence on the House of Commons' terrace was not approved of by all, as the Guardian recorded on 11th June 1976, and is reproduced here with their kind permission:

> ## *Damp MPs lose their berth right*
> *By Simon Hoggart, Political Correspondent*
> A number of MPs were more than a little disgruntled yesterday after finding themselves displaced from marquees on the hallowed ground of the Commons terrace for the Jubilee firework display.
>
> They could stand on the terrace itself on Thursday night in the drizzle, but the long, gaily striped marquees were occupied by about 500 well-off yachtsmen from four different clubs who had been booked for some weeks.
>
> The booking had been made by Dr Reginald Bennett, the Tory MP for Fareham, who is chairman of the catering sub-committee at the Commons. Dr Bennett, an enthusiastic yachtsmen, belongs to two of the clubs and is commodore of one of them, the Imperial Poona Yacht Club. The yachtsmen paid for the use of the terrace; the money would go into House of Commons funds.
>
> The result was that the MPs stood clutching what drink they could find and braving the rain while the water pageant went past and the fireworks went up. Not surprisingly, it was Labour MPs who were most angered by the sight of the yachtsmen. Mr Arthur Latham, a former chairman of the Tribune group, says he will table a Commons motion protesting about "these high class squatters taking over the Palace of Westminster."
>
> Mr Latham went on: "MPs and their guests could not even get a cup of tea because the catering committee had let out accommodation to these clubs. We stood in the rain while the marquees were handed over to these people, suitably furnished with a bar and booth. If we had been displaced by people like pensioners we would not have minded, but to let it out to the most undesirable elements of British Society is too much to stomach."

Raid To Deauville

A fourth raid to Deauville took place in 1976, on board the newly elected John Prentice's 'Battlecry'. It was reported that:

The natives were again friendly, and have proclaimed that in light of these four cultural missions, to say nothing of the occupation of the Pegasus Bridge over the Orne some time before, Normandy, and in particular, Calvados, have returned to the Imperial fold. Cognac and Bordeaux have not yet been reinstated, but efforts will continue.

Prince Philip Pot

We left the Prince Philip Cup in an earlier chapter when it moved to Bembridge in 1973 and expanded to be a championship in keelboats for the twelve sailing clubs based in the Isle of Wight (including Poona).

Poona was not successful in the first year of the new format, but was in 1974. The following year, with only two races held due to strong winds, there was an unbreakable tie for first place between Poona and the Royal Corinthian Yacht Club. The donor commented *"with pots, as with wits, it is better to have half than none."*

Poona was next victorious in 1980.

With the demise of the Bembridge club boats, Noel Dobbs (McPuke) negotiated the transfer of the event to Seaview in 1990, sailed in their Mermaids. In the first year at Seaview, 8 teams competed and Poona won their 10th victory since 1957. This was added to two years later in 1992.

Poona has always strived to maintain the traditions of this unique competition (although it could hardly claim to have become *"the most important series of races in the world"* which Uffa Fox anticipated after the first event). Seaview continue to host the event, and Poona's Peter Hunter has become the Race Officer and ensures the traditions and purpose of the event are upheld.

Sir Hugh Janion

At the end of a successful naval career, Rear-Admiral Sir Hugh Janion was Captain of HM Yacht Britannia for the unusually long period from 1975 to 1981. In this position he got to know Reggie and it was entirely appropriate that he was elected a member of Poona on his retirement, with the title, Colonel-in-Chief, and the name, Sam Pan, Captain of the Heads.

His first role in "civvy street" was when he was asked by the Prince of Wales to handle his wedding presents. An obituary for Hugh recounted:

He had to take on four assistants and eventually sent letters of thanks to the donors of about 6,000 gifts, stored in the cinema of Buckingham Palace, ranging from a solid gold dhow to a book entitled 'Mining in Botswana', and from a heart shaped potato to a Clementi piano.

What this account does not mention is the letter which appeared on his desk from Motilai Banerji Ram, the humble secretary of the Indio-Pakistani Youth Clubs (IPYC) in Peckham and Brixton offering either a Tandori oven or ghari with wheels.

When he realised who this was actually from, Hugh replied that the royal couple would be delighted to accept either gift, but then he got the reply:

Is saddest and ashaming happening destruction of oven for tandoori, alas all bricks stolen and throwing at Constabulary when humble secretariat not looking, also gharri altogether burned up and wheels thrown away by untouchable Harijans from Bangladesh or Peckham extra sadness indeed very sorry.

A few years later, in 1984 (which we will come to soon), Hugh returned to Britannia, drawing from the stores a pair of bell-bottoms and a flannel, a mop and a bucket, which he returned a few days later. This mystified the crew, but history records him in a photograph at the Poona Jubilee, sitting in the front row, equipped as Captain of the Heads, surmounted by a great wide conical Shan State straw hat.

Seaview Buffs

In 1978 the Seaview Buffs, an "inner circle" of the Seaview Yacht Club which is even older than Poona but with a very similar constitution and comparable behaviour, challenged Poona to a match in Mermaids.

This has been repeated ever since and the Thunder Mug is presented to each club alternatively at this match.

This is now the main Poona sailing gathering of the year and consists of a very good dinner on the Saturday night and racing on the Sunday. Not surprisingly, it is an occasion of much merry making and one or two incidents. The author will be accused of censorship if he fails to provide details of one such incident which has become part of Poona folklore.

Allegedly, when the Poona party were walking home after dinner from the club to Peter Hunter's house, a certain person was spotted by the local constabulary relieving himself on the wheel of a parked Seaview bus.

The party then proceeded down the garden path and turned right into the house. However, after a short while, there was a knock on the door. Peter Andreae opened it to find the local bobby demanding to speak to the last person who entered the house. Quick as a flash, Peter said he would willingly collect the said person, who was none other than Rear-Admiral Sir Hugh Janion, late of the Royal Yacht Britannia.

Hugh's experience in dealing with the lower ranks came to the fore as, complete with monocle and dressed in his monogrammed silk dressing gown, he dismissed the constable.

Allegedly, no Poona member lied during this incident, as the last member of the party walking down the path (the Gully Gully Man) had failed to turn right into the house, but had collapsed to the left and was fast asleep in the flowerbed! This left the more respectable, and less inebriated, Sir Hugh as the last person to have entered the house.

Tiffins

Regular Tiffins continued during the 1970s, usually held in London at White's in St James's, but Reggie's knighthood in 1979 demanded a greater celebration. This was held during Cowes Week in the, appropriately named, Durbar Room at Osborne House on the Isle of Wight. This also marked the Club's 45th anniversary. The club returned to the same venue for a Durbar in 1990.

Another notable Durbar was the celebration of the Club's half century in 1984. Sadly someone with celestial authority had left their mark a bit earlier and grabbed the actual anniversary date, 22nd April, as Easter Sunday, so Poona (unusually) held back and celebrated the following weekend.

Durbar Celebrating The Imperial Poona Yacht Club's Golden Jubilee Moundsmere Manor, 27th April, 1984

It was a grand affair at Moundsmere Manor, near Basingstoke, home of Mark Andreae, Fuzzy Wuzzy, who was promptly re-named Cornucopia as a result of his magnificence.

Reggie's invitation promised *"unlimited sherbet and a spectrum of more or less inflammatory curries, together with ghee, dhal, poppadums, chapatti, Bombay Duck and other fauna and flora, at a modest charge not exceeding one lakh of rupees per turban."*

This Durbar was attended by most of the active sahibs, accompanied by memsahibs and camp followers, representatives of many of the overseas outposts and those who had previously been on the active list who were still active enough to attend. Most were, as requested, in oriental dress or yellow and red attire. We have already described Hugh Janion's costume.

An Outpouring Of Outposts

The Home station was beaten to it, by a new outpost, the Middle Kingdom Outpost, or Middle Kingdom Mandarins, which was formed on 22nd April 1984 and had its Inaugural Tiffin at the Royal Hong Kong Yacht Club on the precise day of anniversary.

They were fortunate enough to be entertained to a Tiffin on board Britannia by the Maharaja when he visited Hong Kong in 1987.

Not content with such high honour, the Middle Kingdom outpost also started missionary work. One of its sahibs, Roland Lennox King, moved to New Zealand and found companionship with James Watlington, from the Bermuda outpost, as their new home hosted the America's Cup competition. With Reggie's blessing, on 9th February 1997, they formed the Inverted Colonies Outpost in 1997.

The Club burgee was duly *"hung from the wall not two fathoms from and facing down upon the great Silver Mug."*

Endeavour

1989 saw the renovation of the J-Class yacht Endeavour by Elizabeth Meyer. Involved in this re-fit was Poona member, Riggah, Frank Murdoch. Frank was responsible for the revolutionary rod-rigging, as well as many other unique sailing aids, when this yacht was competing for the Americas Cup back in 1934, and his knowledge was invaluable for the renovation.

He engineered an invitation for the Imperial Poona Yacht Club to sail onboard this magnificent re-launched yacht on 7th July 1989. With a 130ft yacht there was room for the entire Poona membership on the trip, although the author was prevented from attending by the birth of his first child.

Reggie recalls *"beating down past Calshot with the double-clawed jib-topsail set was a stirring experience."* However, there was something missing – the Poona members needed refreshment if this was to be a really memorable Tiffin. Fortunately, a radio message from Hamish Janson (Oont) to the Royal Yacht Squadron saw that club's launch – suitably supplied – rendezvous with Endeavour mid-Solent, and the problem was solved.

I wish I had been there!

The Champagne Arrives For Poona's Outing On Endeavour, 7th July, 1989

More Tiffins

Throughout the 1990s regular Tiffins continued, and the 60th anniversary (1994) was celebrated by a Tiffin at the house of Peter Andreae, Grand Mufti and Finance Member. No less than eleven far-flung representatives of the imperial outposts were present.

In 1997 a Glorious Durbar was held in April at the recently renovated Frogmore House, a Bungalow chosen by the Queen Empress Victoria in which to enjoy her honeymoon. It stands in the grounds of Windsor Castle.

The Maharaja warmly welcomed us, although the staff were later heard to say that they had wished someone had warned them it was a piss-up. They had to go back to the castle three times for more drink!

The Durbar at Frogmore House, Windsor Castle, April 1997

West Country Tour

In 1999, Poona went further and toured the West Country. This involved no less than twelve of the twenty one sahibs considered active at the time, accompanied by memsahibs and camp followers.

The first stop was at Fowey, where we competed against the Troy Class, sailing from the Fowey Gallants Sailing Club. That evening, a Tiffin was organised at the Royal Fowey Yacht Club from whence to bed.

The next morning we travelled to Falmouth where the intention was to race against the sublimely named Falmouth Artisan's River Training Squadron (FARTS, for short) in the classic working oyster-boats of the Truro River. Sadly, the tides did not co-operate, and so we dined at The Ganges Restaurant at Mylor instead.

That afternoon we travelled to the Pendennis Yard in Falmouth to see the Commode's old ship, Shamrock V, which had just arrived for a refit. Reggie was clearly in his element as he checked out his old boat from over sixty years previously, recalling the uneven deck and other details.

THE NEW MILLENIUM

The Founder Dies

The last Tiffin Reggie attended was on 26th July 2000 at Whites, in the presence of the Maharaja. Sadly in September 2000 Reggie became ill and was admitted to Charing Cross Hospital. After two and a half months he moved to a nursing home in part of what was once the Royal Masonic Hospital at Hammersmith.

Despite being very ill, weak, and mentally confused, Reggie had not stopped thinking imperially and was concerned about the future of the Imperial Poona Yacht Club. He made several attempts to write to the Maharaja about the continuation of the Club, but finally it was left to Henrietta, Reggie's wife, to write to this effect. He wanted the Maharaja to help select a new Commode.

Reggie died on 19th December 2000 and this was greeted with great sadness by both the sailing and political communities. This history started with his obituary, and it is not necessary to report all the tributes, but Ian Wooldridge's words in the Daily Mail are worth recording:

> *Arrivederci, Reggie*
>
> *A lovely, irreplaceable character died this week and I write with great respect of Reggie Bennett, more formally known for 24 years as Sir Reginald Bennett MP.*
>
> *He portrayed all his austere Wykehamist education by hugely enjoying yachting, long lunches and public life, roughly in that order.*
>
> *He was wonderful company and had packed in about 150 years of life before his death at the age on 89.*

Picking Up The Pieces

Peter Hunter, the Great White Vice, was at home when the phone rang and the voice at the other end informed him they were calling from Buckingham Palace. He nearly replied that he was the Queen of Sheeba when it became clear that the Maharaja was fulfilling Reggie's wishes and urging Poona to continue and elect a replacement for him

A Tiffin was held in April 2001 at the Royal Thames Yacht Club and the future was much discussed. Should Reggie's resignation under Rule 9 (a) [death] be refused, as had been the case for The Commodore of the Repulsive But Not Revolting Outpost, Bill Gooderham?

In the end, it was decided to elect Reggie as the Celestial Commode and Peter Hunter would become the Terrestrial Commode.

(Because of Hunter's appalling spelling, this was initially written as Terrestial Commode, but fortunately this was corrected by Buckingham Palace!). Malcolm Green was elevated from Great Gorgeous Rear to Great White Vice, and Ben Vines was elected Great Gorgeous Rear.

The Poona Team at Seaview in 2007

New Blood

Ben Vines was part of a group of young sailors who Reggie had prompted the Club to elect after the 50th anniversary. These included Ben, Andrew Green and Ed Smith who had all been in the British Universities' Sailing Team which had toured the United States in 1995.

Their election was felt to *"greatly increase the credibility of the Poona Teams in world-class events such as the Prince Philip Pot, and will be able to represent Poona in events far and wide."*

Their election, and that of other younger members, soon had the anticipated effect, winning the Prince Philip Pot in 1998, 1999, 2002, 2003, 2004 and 2005.

Andrew Green also became very active on the Match Racing circuit and won the Royal Bermuda Yacht Club's Gold Cup for Poona in 1999 – the first time for 40 years it had been in English hands.

A Poona team also started entering major team racing events, in 2004 reaching the quarter finals of the Wilson Trophy.

Not So Young Blood

But the younger members of the club did not grab all the sailing headlines for Poona. In 2006 Abdul Gunneybags set out on his second solo round the world trip, this time stopping, in his boat, who's Poona name was Sagah In-Shore Ranse, competing in the Velux 5 Oceans Race.

He received a message shortly before the start of the race:

*Now to Abdul we cheer, As
we down a large beer,
While Sagah sets her sails,
With a man hard as nails,
And Hot Chilli Sauce,
To complete his resource,
So we sing to the skies
As the ocean he flies:*

*The sons of the Prophet are brave men and bold
And quite unaccustomed to fear,
But the bravest by far in the ranks of the Shah,
Was Abdul Abulbul Amir.*

*If you wanted a man to encourage the van,
Or harass the foe from the rear,
Storm fort or redoubt, you had only to shout
For Abdul Abulbul Amir.*

*Salaams and Salutations, may the Great Gods bless you,
From the Massed Ranks of POONA Sahibs.*

Robin finished third in this race – a great achievement for someone 67 years young!

Tiffins

While Reggie's presence always guaranteed a good party, his absence has not prevented Poona from continuing to have them.

At the Regatta in 2001 to celebrate the 150th anniversary of the first Americas Cup race in Cowes, a memorable Tiffin was held at the Irrigation Fellah's house in Cowes, attended by the Maharaja.

Regular Tiffins are held during Cowes Week, often at John Terry's Commodore's House, and in 2008 the Maharaja invited the sahibs to drinks on board THV Galatea, the new Trinity House Vessel.

In March 2006 there was a Tiffin at the Royal Thames Yacht Club to celebrate 50th anniversary of Prince Philip Pot, with the donor present.

And So To 75 Years

This book is published as Poona celebrates the 75th anniversary of its founding. Not bad for a Club which was actually disbanded after four years because *"it had served its purpose."*

A hint of the reason for its longevity was provided in the newspaper article about the first races against the Revolting Colonists in 1951: *"The reason for it has gone, but the spirit and comradeship have survived."*

It is a totally unique club, with a limited, but surprisingly diverse, membership, who enjoy each other's company.

It is undoubtedly true that, without Reggie, it has lost his magic. People also have less time available now for the more frivolous things in life, and, with only twenty five members, events need well over half of them attending, which is not easily achieved. But when they do happen, the magic returns and some members are even capable of speech, as the rules say they may be!

Chota Hazri!

FLAG OFFICERS

Commodore

1934-38	Sir Archibald Hope	1946-2000	Sir Reginald Bennett

Celestial Commode

2001-   Sir Reginald Bennett

Terrestrial Commode

2001-   Peter Hunter

Great White Vice

1934-38	Charles Johnston	1998-2001	Peter Hunter
1946-70	Sir Heneage Ogilvie	2001-	Prof Sir Malcolm Green
1970-82	Charles Blake		
1982-98	Brian Appleton		

Great Black Vice

1970-81   Stephen Longsdon

Great Gorgeous Rear

1934-38	Roy Mitchell	1982-98	Peter Hunter
1946-49	Stephen Longsdon	1998-2001	Malcolm Green
1949-55	John Palmer	2001-	Ben Vines
1955-82	John Chamier		

Colonel-in-Chief

1934-62	Tiny Mitchell	1991-94	Rear Admiral Sir Hugh Janion
1968-70	Sir Heneage Ogilvie		
1973-90	Sir Alec Rose	2010-	Sir Robin Knox-Johnston

Secretariat-Wallah

1934	JHM Rabone	1966-67	Stephen Longsdon
1934-36	Arthur Whitehead	1968	Peter Andreae
1946	Reggie Bennett	1969-74	Nevill Ambler
1946-47	Cecil Knight	1974-2009	Prof Sir Malcolm Green
1949	Reggie Bennett		
1949-66	Hugh Somerville	2010-	Jeremy Atkins

www.ingramcontent.com/pod-product-compliance
Lightning Source LLC
Chambersburg PA
CBHW050605300426
44112CB00013B/2088